PADDY MULLINS

PADDY MULLINS

THE MASTER OF DONINGA

The Authorised Biography

Peter O'Neill and Sean Boyne

Foreword by Peter O'Sullevan

MAINSTREAM
PUBLISHING

EDINBURGH AND LONDON

First published in Great Britain in 1995 by
MAINSTREAM PUBLISHING COMPANY (EDINBURGH) LTD
7 Albany Street
Edinburgh EH1 3UG

ISBN 1 85158 748 9

A catalogue record for this book is available from the British Library

Typeset in Sabon
Printed and bound in Great Britain by Butler & Tanner Ltd, Frome

Contents

Acknowledgments

The authors would like to thank all those who helped with this book, especially Paddy Mullins, who gave generously of his time, who talked to us honestly and frankly, and without whom there would be no book. We would like to thank his wife Maureen for her help in persuading Paddy to go against the self-effacing instincts of a lifetime and to go along with the idea for this biography. We are grateful for her help and co-operation in sharing her memories with us and for giving us access to files and research material. We would also like to thank the other members of the Mullins family who shared their thoughts and memories with us – Tony, Willy, Tom, George, Sandra and Sandra's husband Peter McCarthy.

Our thanks must also go to the others who were kind enough to give us interviews – Terry Casey, John Clarke, Sarah Daniels, Eddie Hayden, Paddy Kehoe, Andrew MacMurrough Kavanagh, Christy Maye, Stan Mellor, Sheila Moore, Mohammed Mubarak, Jim Murphy, David Nicholson, Clody Norton, Margaret O'Leary, Jonjo O'Neill and Dr Malcolm Thorpe.

We are grateful to Michael Brophy, Managing Director of *Sunday World* for assistance with computer facilities, and also to Stephen Cranley, whose computer expertise was a great help. We would also like to thank *Sunday World* photographer Liam O'Connor for his assistance. We are grateful to racing photographers Liam Healy and Caroline Norris for their co-operation and for their kind permission to use their photographs.

Research in the files of the *Irish Field* was vital to the project and we would like to thank the Editor, Valentine Lamb, for his very valuable assistance. Our thanks also to Michael O'Connor of the *Irish Field*.

Peter O'Sullevan was most helpful and encouraging – we are most grateful.

Foreword

A man for all seasons is Paddy Mullins – a master of his craft as quietly effective at preparing the winner of the Champion Stakes (Hurry Harriet) as the Champion Hurdle (Dawn Run). It is presumptuous on my part but I suspect that Paddy and I share a common attitude in that we would both prefer to try and do our respective jobs than to talk about them. The difference is that Paddy would have a great deal more to talk about!

For more than 40 years Patrick Mullins – founder, with his delightful wife, Maureen, of a remarkable racing dynasty – has been at the forefront of his profession. There would have been an unacceptable void in the literature of the Turf had not Sean Boyne and Peter O'Neill chronicled the Paddy Mullins story.

With admiration and gratitude they record the realisation of their subject's triumphs from, 'Punchestown to Paris; from Clonmel to Camden, North Carolina; from Wexford to Maisons-Laffitte; from Sligo to Sandown and from Limerick to Longchamp.'

I had the privilege in 1968 of 'calling' Paddy's first Cheltenham Festival winner Herring Gull (who beat Gay Trip six lengths in the Tote Champion Novices Chase) and, later, both legs of Dawn Run's historic Champion/Gold Cup double.

It is a privilege for me to commend the story of the elder statesman of his profession – a gentle man in every sense.

Prologue

It should have been the most joyous, the most triumphant moment of his professional career. But instead Paddy Mullins, the quiet man of Irish racing, had just an overwhelming feeling of emptiness. It was just after the mare he had trained to perfection, Dawn Run, had won the Gold Cup at Cheltenham in March 1986. All Ireland was ecstatic, for the gallant Irish mare, ridden by Corkman Jonjo O'Neill, entered the history books that day. She became the only racehorse yet to win two of the most coveted prizes in National Hunt racing —the Gold Cup and the Champion Hurdle.

Yet, on that memorable day, Paddy Mullins was haunted by the feeling that he had been made to sacrifice his own son Tony to achieve that great victory. Tony Mullins was the number one jockey at the Mullins stable near Goresbridge, Co. Kilkenny. He had achieved a remarkable six wins in succession on Dawn Run. Yet everyone knew that the owner of Dawn Run, the formidable Mrs Charmian Hill, wanted a 'more experienced' rider to partner the mare in the major races. Some weeks before the Gold Cup, Paddy had sent out Tony to ride Dawn Run at Cheltenham in a 'prep race' for the big event. The mare had not yet perfected her technique as a 'chaser, and Tony took a fall. Paddy felt, however, that the experience on the day played a vital role in paving the way for the Gold Cup win. Yet, having sent his son Tony out to take the knocks, he was not permitted to let him take the glory on the big day itself.

Paddy Mullins was convinced that the mare ran better for Tony than for anybody else – even for riders who had more experience. Despite this view as a professional, he knew that if he were to insist on Tony riding the mare, it would be seen as simply a father trying to do a favour for his son. He was in a classic 'no-win' situation. Mrs Hill would probably have preferred to have ridden Dawn Run in the Gold Cup herself. She was devastated some years previously when the Turf Club decided that, at the age of 62, the 'galloping granny' was too old to continue riding Dawn Run – or any other horse – in races. Perhaps she resented the idea of a young chap like Tony, who was only in his early twenties, taking her seat on her beloved mare. At the end of the day, no matter what processes were going on in her mind, she didn't want Tony. And thus it came about that it was Jonjo O'Neill, not Tony Mullins, who was in the saddle when Dawn Run won both the Champion Hurdle and the Gold Cup. To have two such wins on the one horse is the stuff of which jockeys' dreams are made – and it was a real letdown for Tony Mullins to be 'jocked off' the mare and to lose those two rides. It was always his dream to ride a winner at Cheltenham – a dream that will never now be realised, for he gave up riding some years ago due to injury.

And so it was that when the vast crowd at Cheltenham went wild with delight after the Gold Cup win, Paddy Mullins and his wife Maureen, felt no emotion at all. The final act in the tragedy was the death of Dawn Run who, in the words of a *Racing Post* tribute, was 'killed in action on the fields of France' later that year. Paddy had not wanted to send Dawn Run to the French Champion Hurdle, since the mare had been schooled to jump fences rather than the difficult French hurdles. But the owner wanted to send the mare to Paris – and she didn't want to send Tony either. Dawn Run, ridden by a French jockey, fell and broke her neck. John Clarke, the lad who normally looked after Dawn Run, was at home in Ireland due to an injury and he has described how he wept when he heard the news. His reaction was not untypical. In the eyes of many back in Ireland, Dawn Run had assumed the proportions of a national heroine and her followers were virtually in mourning after her premature demise.

For the Mullins family, the Dawn Run saga meant joy at first – it's marvellous for any stable to have a horse in a million like 'the mare', as she was always called. But in the long run, more than anything, it meant anguish. The matter is not discussed in the family circle to this day. There are too many painful memories. And yet, throughout the entire saga, Paddy Mullins never had a row with Mrs Hill. Each knew what the other's position was, but their differences never spilled over into confrontation. There are those who may be surprised to learn that, despite all the problems and all the pain, owner and trainer always maintained a mutual respect for one another. Paddy Mullins today makes it clear that he still has the height of respect and regard for the late Mrs Hill, as a person – and as an owner.

Paddy Mullins, very much the senior statesman of Irish racing having been involved in training for more than a half century, has learned wisdom over the decades. In the Dawn Run affair, he feels he was merely the victim of what might be termed 'the curse of the good horse'. He has seen it happen before – all goes smoothly, perhaps for many years, with an owner. Then a really good horse comes along, and soon the difficulties start. There is no shortage of instant experts on racing and the owner of a good horse will find himself or herself bombarded with 'advice' from all directions – 'advice' that often runs contrary to that offered by the real professional involved – the trainer. Or the 'advice' might be to send the horse to another stable.

Every trainer wants to have that really good horse in his yard – but sometimes that 'good horse' can prove to be a poisoned chalice. In the earlier part of his training career, there was a 'good horse' in Paddy's yard called Height O'Fashion. The horse brought in its wake difficulties with the owner. Paddy felt the owner was listening to outsiders instead of listening to him. On this occasion the Goresbridge trainer took drastic action – he put his livelihood at risk by telling the owner to take all his horses away. He has mellowed since then.

Paddy Mullins is a shy, soft-spoken man, who has always shunned the limelight. He has always preferred to let his horses do his talking for him. He is the most unflamboyant of men and was never one who sought out the more showy aspects of the racing world – the big-time gambling, the glittering parties, the champagne receptions. With people whom he knows and likes, he is great company and a great raconteur. But to the outside world he is a man of few words who tends to avoid the media. It is clear, however, that beneath the self-effacing exterior is a man with a rare genius to train horses, a genius that stems partly from an uncanny rapport with the animal world. It is a genius that has made Paddy Mullins the leading National Hunt trainer in Ireland.

Now in his mid-seventies, Paddy Mullins can look back on a brilliant career filled with achievements, at home and abroad. Apart from his unequalled record at Cheltenham with Dawn Run, his tally includes four wins in the Irish Grand National and, on the Flat, a win in the prestigious Champion Stakes at Newmarket. He is the only trainer from Britain or Ireland ever to win the French Champion Hurdle, and he also won the richest jump race ever held in the world, the $750,000 Dueling Grounds International Hurdle which was run at Bowling Green, Kentucky in 1990. In Leopardstown that same year, for the second year in succession, he sent out Redundant Pal to win Europe's richest handicap hurdle race, the Ladbroke. In addition, there has been a huge tally of wins in more modest events, resulting in him being declared, for many years in succession, Ireland's champion National Hunt trainer.

He has always had a particular ability with mares, and some of these mares have recorded marvellous wins for him. One thinks in particular of Dawn Run; of Hurry Harriet who won the Champion Stakes, and Grabel, who won the Dueling Grounds race and amassed more prize money than any other Irish National Hunt horse. In the human sphere, some of his most important owners have also belonged to the female of the species.

14

From modest beginnings, through hard work and perseverance that kept him going through the good times and the bad, and with the aid of his wife Maureen, he made it as a trainer. He has been involved in training for an incredible period of more than 55 years, working at first for others and then operating under his own name. He has had a trainer's licence for 42 years. He is still going strong at his yard in Doninga, where, in his quiet way, he is very much in charge and where he is always known simply as 'the boss'. All of his five children have inherited his passion for horses and they all make their living from the Irish horse industry. Paddy and Maureen Mullins have founded a veritable dynasty that must be almost unique in the racing world. Paddy and his wife, his four sons, daughter, son-in-law and two daughters-in-law have something in common – all ten have ridden winners under National Hunt rules. Two of his sons are successful trainers while a third is his assistant trainer.

Paddy has been so long in the business that one finds that many of today's prominent trainers, including David 'The Duke' Nicholson, once rode for him as jockeys. And he has seen during his career a most varied array of horses – and of owners – come and go. Going through the names of his owners at random, you will find here a titled lady from the English aristocracy, there a Country and Western singer, or an Indian business tycoon, or a well-known high-rolling gambler, or a mega-rich brother-in-law of the Crown Prince of Saudi Arabia, or a mysterious Hong Kong millionaire who only communicates by fax. Among his owners, all human life is there.

From his yard at Doninga, Paddy Mullins has sent thousands of horses out to compete at home and abroad. He has had runners on every racecourse in Ireland and has won on every track except Downpatrick and Laytown. He has decades of experience in sending out horses to compete in many far-flung foreign fields as well. The horses of Doninga have seen action from Punchestown to Paris; from Clonmel to Camden, North Carolina; from Wexford to Washington DC; from

Mallow to Maisons-Laffitte; from Sligo to Sandown and from Limerick to Longchamp.

In April 1995, the Mullins-trained Boro Eight, ridden by Norman Williamson, made a late, unexpected challenge to finish a close second to the wonder horse Danoli in the Martell Aintree Hurdle. The impressive performance of Boro Eight impelled former top jockey Peter Scudamore to pay a memorable compliment to the wily old Master of Doninga. Said Scudamore, while commentating for BBC TV, 'Paddy Mullins, you can never write him off. He doesn't bring horses over here for the good of his health. He is a master of his trade . . .'

There are few who will argue with that assessment. After literally decades of working with horses, decades of meticulous attention to detail, decades of sticking with his vocation through thick and thin, Paddy Mullins can surely be described as a master of his trade . . .

CHAPTER 1

A Happy Childhood

Paddy Mullins had an idyllic childhood. There was political turmoil in Ireland at the time of his birth on 28 January 1919 but the tensions that were shortly to explode into insurrection and civil war impinged very little on the baby born into a farming family in Co. Kilkenny. Looking back on his early years so many decades ago, Paddy Mullins realises now just how broadly fortune had smiled upon him as a child. Born in Old Grange, near the village of Graiguenamanagh, the family moved in December 1923 to another farm some miles away which had been bought by his grandfather, James Mullins. Around this period he can remember people talking about roads being blown up and cratered – obviously as a result of the civil war – and this is his earliest memory. His brother Jim, who was a year and a half older, could in later years recall seeing heavily armed men near the family farm. These were the Black and Tans, members of the force used by the British authorities to fight the Irish Republican rebels of that era. But politics and rebellion and civil war seemed very far away indeed as the young Paddy Mullins settled in at the marvellous country estate which his family had just acquired.

The family's new home was an elegant Georgian residence, Doninga House, close by the banks of the River Barrow, near the village of Goresbridge. The English writer Thackeray had stayed there in 1842. The holding was sizeable, the land was good and Paddy's father Willie was a good farmer. For a child, growing up on the farm at Doninga was like living in a rural wonderland. Doninga House, with its surrounding parkland and woodlands, had been originally designed as the rural retreat of a gentleman. The Mullins farm fronted, for about a mile, the broad sweep of the River Barrow, one of the great rivers of the ancient Irish province of Leinster. There was good trout fishing in the river and there were marvellous places too where one could go swimming. There was a view across to the hills of the Mount Leinster range and on the farm, set in gently undulating wooded countryside, there were always ponies and horses.

The love and knowledge of horses was in the Mullins family for generations. Paddy's father and grandfather were horsemen, who were both involved in the breeding and training of horses, especially hunters. Paddy can just about remember his grandfather, who had been born just after the Famine of the late 1840s and who had farmed at Knockadereen, Co. Kilkenny. Horses raised by the Mullins family in generations past were sold off for use as cavalry horses abroad in an era when armies still had mounted units. There has been a long tradition of Irish horses going to foreign armies. Napoleon's white charger Marengo was bred in Kilmuckridge, Co. Wexford, while the Duke of Wellington's black charger Copenhagen was bought at Cahirmee Fair in Co. Cork, a fair that is held to this day.

Willie Mullins, Paddy's father, also trained racehorses, and the skills involved have passed naturally to his son, as indeed the skills have been passed on by Paddy to his own sons. Horses have been the passion of Paddy Mullins from as far back as he can remember. He may be famous for his reticence and he may be shy and reserved with people whom he does not know, but there are no such barriers when Paddy Mullins comes to dealing with the creatures of the equine world. He has an uncanny rapport with them, a rapport that has helped him become a legend as a National Hunt trainer. Today, close on three quarters of a century after he moved to the area, Paddy Mullins still lives at Doninga, close by the old family home where he lived as a child. Every night, before he retires to bed, the last thing he does is tour his stables, checking out his charges, ensuring that all is well with them. It is almost impossible to imagine him living a life without his horses.

By the relative standards of the 1920s, the Mullins family was prosperous but times were still hard. Money was in short supply during those tough years in the aftermath of the First World War. Paddy was one of seven children. Large families were the norm in the strongly Catholic Ireland of those times. Willie Mullins and his wife, the former Catherine Hayden, had four boys when the family lived at Old Grange and after moving to Doninga, three girls were born. Paddy believes his family is of French origin. They had originally lived in the Wexford area but had moved to the lush green pastures of Co. Kilkenny some time after the 1798 rebellion.

There are local folk memories to do with the rebellion – and they involve horses too. Not far from Doninga, there was a big massacre of rebels at a ford on the River Barrow. The soldiers chased one man whom they took to be a rebel into a local farmhouse where he was employed as a labourer. The soldiers pointed to the man's wet boots and said this was a sign he had been out early in the morning, taking part in the fighting. A young man in the household managed to avert the labourer's summary execution by explaining that the man had been out in the fields after the family's horses. A grandson of that young man, Jack Donohoe, was later to be the first significant owner to send his horses to Paddy Mullins when the Doninga trainer was trying to build up his business in the early 1960s.

One of the country pursuits in this part of Ireland over the generations was fox hunting and this provided a point of contact between the farmers and the landed Anglo-Irish gentry who lived in the big houses of the region. The hunts traditionally had provided an impetus to point-to-point racing across the Irish countryside and these activities in turn helped to provide a foundation for the National Hunt races over hurdles and fences that we know today. Some farmers would supplement their agricultural income by breeding, raising, training and stabling horses earmarked for hunting or point-to-point racing and Paddy's father Willie was one such farmer.

Willie was friendly with Major Dermot McCalmont of Mount Juliet estate, a landowner who was also deeply involved in the Kilkenny Hunt. McCalmont would often call on Willie's skills as a mediator if any local farmer had a grievance against the hunt. Paddy recalls with a grin, 'If a cow was injured or lost her calf as a result of the hunt passing through a farmer's land, somehow it would always happen to be the best one the farmer had. Very often a dispute would be settled by taking a cow out of the Mount Juliet estate and replacing the lost cow. And you could be sure that at the next fair day in Kilkenny that new cow would be out for sale.'

Willie Mullins was also a respected figure in local racing circles and was a founding member of the committee of the local Gowran Park racecourse when it was set up in 1914. Paddy recalls how there were always horses around the family farm. 'People would send us horses to break and to hunt and to sell on, and my father would buy the odd horse to be made and sold on. There would always be somebody around the place, like Paddy Curran, helping my father to do the rough stuff. I would be assisting and observing and gradually learned how to break horses. My father also bred horses – these were mostly half-breds at the time. We would breed hunters – there were one or two thoroughbred mares but that was all. We would rear them and sell them on.'

Paddy Mullins recalls how a bloodstock agent from Switzerland would come to the area to buy horses, some of whom would be destined for the Swiss army. The agent was Max Hauri and he would base himself at a farm owned by the Hughes family near Gowran. Paddy remembers as a youngster bringing horses to that farm to show to the agent with a view to selling them. Decades later, Max Hauri's son, a leading Swiss showjumper and horse dealer, would have racehorses in training with Paddy Mullins. And Paddy's son Tom married Helen Hughes, a sister of leading Irish showjumper Marion Hughes, granddaughters of the man who had the farm where Max Hauri bought the horses.

Paddy Mullins and his father kept their horses in the old

stables beside Doninga House – the same stables that the writer William Makepeace Thackeray described in his acclaimed work *The Irish Sketchbook*. The book was written following Thackeray's four-month tour of Ireland in the summer and winter of 1842, and he describes how he spent a memorable night in the house of D—, which has been identified as the old house that later became the residence of the Mullins family.

Thackeray describes how a 'young son of the house', on a white pony, was on the look-out for the coach carrying the writer and his fellow passengers. 'Trotting away by the carriage-side, he brought us through a gate with a pretty avenue of trees leading to the pleasure-grounds of the house – a handsome building commanding noble views of river, mountains and plantations.' Later, after some excellent hospitality and dancing, and it being a fine night, the young squire who rented the house brought Thackeray out to the stables to smoke cigars and to show the English writer a fine mare by the light of a lantern. Who knows? Perhaps that mare was the ancestor of some of the horses that were to inhabit those very same stables at the time of the Mullins family.

Paddy has read Thackeray's account of Doninga and says the description of the stables tallies exactly with the way he remembers them when he was a child and later when he started training. Thackeray also described how he spent the night in a coaching hotel at Royal Oak, a tiny hamlet a few miles from Doninga. The original building, although in ruins, survived until about 20 years ago when it was demolished. Paddy's wife Maureen was anguished to see it go. She recalls how, on the day it was due to be knocked down, she took a photo of the old hotel on her way to a race meeting in Fairyhouse. On her way home that evening, not a stone remained.

If the ghost of Thackeray had returned to Doninga House some 90 years after his original visit, he would again have encountered a young boy on a pony, just like the young boy who had welcomed him in 1842. From his most tender years, the young Paddy Mullins was riding ponies. He was taking part in showjumping events and riding in children's pony races. In

1931, at the age of 11, he won his first race, a children's point-to-point, riding a little pony called Bobby. He still remembers the excitement of winning that first race. It was held at Old Grange and nobody fancied his chances and even though there were bookmakers present, there were no bets on the Mullins boy. Paddy Curran, the jockey who helped his father with the horses, helped him that day by edging the pony forward a little before the start. Says Paddy, 'It was a great feeling to win, a hell of a feeling. Despite the winners I have had since, that first win has always rated highly in my memory – especially since I was regarded as a no-hoper.'

Paddy still has the trophy he won that day. It's a tiny cup, but it has its own proud place on a sideboard in the long drawing room of the Mullins residence, not far from mementos of far more august victories, in events such as the Cheltenham Gold Cup. Paddy Curran, the man who helped him the day he won the cup, had previously ridden for John Kirwan, the local trainer. Paddy Curran was the father of Matt Curran who was later to ride two Irish Grand National winners for the Mullins stable, Dim Wit and Vulpine. Says Paddy Mullins, 'Paddy Curran's grandsons are working for me still. Sean Curran who came over to ride for me in the Ladbroke in 1995, is one of them as well – a son of Matt's.' In this business, in an area like Goresbridge, inter-family links are important and they often continue over the generations.

Apart from horses and ponies, the River Barrow, flowing as it did along by the Mullins farm, was another big source of recreation for the Mullins children. Paddy and the other children and their friends fished for trout and perch and also swam in the river. He particularly remembers the swimming during the summer, when young people from all over the district would gravitate towards the Mullins farm for a 'dip' in the Barrow. Paddy learned to swim in traditional rural style by floating out into the river holding a bundle of bull rushes tied together with twine. He says now, so many years on, 'Swimming and fishing and riding ponies – it was a marvellous childhood. My mother used to warn me that this won't last.

Life was too good, I suppose.' The other pleasures of his childhood were also simple ones – a trip by bicycle to Bagenalstown to the cinema, or 'picture house' as it was called, and card games in the evenings when neighbours would drop in.

Even though Paddy came from a county where Gaelic games – mainly hurling – had a fanatical following, he could never summon up much interest. If the event didn't involve a creature with four legs, he found it a bore. Horses were what he found exciting. He attended the De La Salle Brothers school in Bagenalstown, cycling the four miles there every day. He stayed until the Leaving Certificate exams, then left at the age of 17. It was that same year he began riding in point-to-point races and as far as he was concerned the thrill, the challenge, the drama of the race made football or hurling dull by comparison.

He admits that he did pick up a hurley now and then while at school and hurled 'with the lads' but never in any serious competitive way. He recalls how on one occasion he and other boys from the school were taken to see a football match in Baltinglass, Co. Wicklow, on a bitterly cold day in late October. A team from his own school was playing Belcamp College from Dublin. It was not exactly the most inspiring outing of his life. If he was ever tempted to take an interest in football, that trip to Baltinglass 'cured' him of any such inclination. Although he would, of course, be well-disposed towards Kilkenny on their forays into the All-Ireland hurling finals, he has never actually been to Croke Park to see his county team play in the big event. 'Horses have always been totally my interest,' he says.

One of the factors that sustained his interest in horses was hunting. The Mount Loftus Harriers was established in his area in 1931 and Paddy believes his own involvement in the hunt was a key reason why he became horse-minded. In 1933 the Mount Loftus Harriers established point-to-point races – another outlet for Paddy's burgeoning equestrian skills. Within a couple of years, he was a skilled rider in the point-to-points himself. The Mount Loftus was essentially a farmers' hunt. Many of the younger farmers, like Paddy and his brothers, did not bother with the fancy hunt gear common in some hunts. They wore cloth caps and, later, bowler hats. Paddy's father, however, always wore the traditional hunting outfit.

One of the key figures in the running of the hunt was Major Arthur MacMurrough Kavanagh from Borris, Co. Carlow. The major was a member of the land-owning gentry and traced his ancestry back to the ancient native Irish kings of Leinster. His ancestor was Diarmuid MacMurrough Kavanagh, the twelfth-century King of Leinster who played a key role in bringing the Norman invader Strongbow to Ireland.

The Master of the Mount Loftus Harriers was Dr Bill O'Brien, who brought a pack of hounds with him when he was transferred to the dispensary at Graiguenamanagh. Another leading figure in the hunt was the local racehorse trainer, John Kirwan. The hunt kennels were at Mount Loftus House, Gowran, home of the Loftus family who also kept some hunt horses. This was in the centre of the area where the harriers hunted. (The Loftus estate had links with horses going back generations. Among the subscribers to the *Irish Racing Calendar* for 1790 was listed Nicholas Loftus Esq., Mount Loftus, Gowran.)

Paddy's father Willie was also deeply involved in the hunt, and the Mount Loftus point-to-points were held on the Mullins family farm at Doninga and over a number of neighbouring farms. Willie organised the races himself but by doing it as a one-man operation, Paddy reckons he probably made more enemies than friends. In the 1950s, Willie Mullins was to become joint Master of the hunt, along with Terence Vigors, of nearby Burgage Stud, whose family was very prominent in the bloodstock industry.

Huge crowds would turn out for the point-to-point races, although they were never held on a Sunday in those days. Paddy recalls the old-style point-to-points. 'It wasn't a question of going around two fields like it is now – they went the full three and a half miles through the open country over banks and bushes. With the exception of the foot and mouth year in 1941, the races were held every year until 1955. The hunt closed down around this time, because those who were the mainstay of it had died or faded away.' In 1995 Paddy came across a 1938 photo featuring members of the Mount Loftus Harriers – only two were still alive.

Paddy recalls how on one occasion a 'woman' calling herself Miss Kealy entered for a ladies point-to-point at Doninga. Miss Kealy arrived for the race well made-up and sporting an attractive hairstyle, although there were those who thought the rider looked a little masculine. It was a race for cobs, 15 hands high, and Miss Kealy won easily. It was only some days later that the truth was revealed – 'Miss Kealy' was, in fact, a man. Says Paddy, 'The "lady" turned out to be Jack Kealy. Jack died some time ago, God rest him, and I believe it was done for a joke.

'In a race against ladies, the strength of a man would be worth about two stone or more, so Jack had a big advantage. A hairdresser in Kilkenny did a great job on his coiffure and cosmetics had been used to make him look like a woman. I thought there was something strange about the rider but I was as much caught out as anyone. Within a week everyone knew what had happened and it was the talk of the entire area. No official action was ever taken – I suppose officialdom never likes to be caught out!'

From the 1930s onwards, the young Paddy Mullins was a keen participant in hunt activities. He rode not only with the Mount Loftus Harriers but also with the Carlow and Kilkenny hunts. He sometimes hunted as often as three times a week, and at one stage, for a year, he was the whipper-in for the Mount Loftus hunt. He recalls with nostalgia the joy of the hunt on a fine, crisp, autumn day as the horses and hounds took off across the green, rolling fields of the Carlow-Kilkenny borderlands. 'On a hunting morning I would get up on my horse here in Doninga, trot to the kennels which were about three miles away, and the kennel man would let out the hounds. Then off we'd go to the hunt with the hounds following behind. Of course they would digress a bit if they smelt something. In fact they were notorious going through the village of Gowran. They would go in the back door of a house and out the front, and sometimes come out with a loaf of bread.'

In those days, only the gentry had horse boxes, so the vast majority of people would hack to the hunt. Members of the Catholic clergy would also take part, including the parish priest of Graiguenamanagh and the curate in Paulstown. Paddy enjoyed hunting enormously and describes it as good, innocent fun. He maintains the anti-blood sports people have painted an unfair picture of what it's all about. 'I hunted for 30 years, and I could count the number of kills I saw on one hand. This allegation of "tearing foxes to bits" – that's twisted. I haven't hunted for 20 years, but it's because I could not make the time.'

It was at a Mount Loftus Harriers event, held on the Mullins family farm at Doninga, that Paddy won his first point-to-point. The year was 1942. Having started riding in point-to-points six years previously, he had gradually built up his skills. He would ride his own family horses and also horses for other owners and for the local trainer John Kirwan. He remembers well the details of that first point-to-point win. The horse was owned by Dr Paddy Heffernan from Kilkenny who was the head of one of the many sanatoria that had been established in Ireland in that era due to the TB problem. He kept a lot of horses on a farm in Co. Tipperary and would put some of them into training. Altogether, Paddy was to notch up about 25 winners as a rider in point-to-point events. By the time he retired as a jockey in 1959, he had to his credit 14 victories as an amateur under Rules, winning on the Flat, over hurdles and in 'chases.

Meanwhile, he was moving into training. As he says himself, over a number of years during the 1940s, he gradually 'crept into it'. He had an association with the trainer John Kirwan, who had stables about three miles from Doninga. Kirwan was regarded locally as a very decent man. He was quite successful at the time and he gave the young Paddy Mullins all the assistance he could. The first horses Paddy trained were point-to-pointers and they were trained under the Kirwan licence. These early efforts at training were carried out at Kirwan's stables. Kirwan had been training a long time – in his early years he would charge an owner 2/6 (12.5p) a week for keeping a horse.

Paddy recalls that one of the better horses in training with John Kirwan back in the 1940s was Hatton's Grace. The shrewd Kirwan had a good eye for horses and bought Hatton's Grace as a yearling in 1941 at the Ballsbridge Sales for a mere 18 guineas. Kirwan had an instinct for a bargain – as Paddy Mullins was to have himself during his own career. Hatton's Grace was the horse that was later to go on, under the tutelage of Vincent O'Brien, to win the Champion Hurdle at Cheltenham three years in a row, in 1949, 1950 and 1951. Recalls Paddy, 'I remember seeing him regularly in the field where they galloped the horses, as a yearling, a two-year-old and a three-year-old. He was the apple of Kirwan's eye. He was referred to as "His Gracehorse" because he was by His Grace. When he went into training he was brilliant. The late Colonel Dan Corry, the show jumper, bought him. The horse won with Kirwan and Corry took him out and sent him to the trainer Barney Nugent, Pat Taaffe's uncle.' Under the ownership of Mrs Moya Keogh, the horse was sent to Vincent O'Brien, and then came the historic 'three in a row' at Cheltenham.

Apart from those early visits to the Kirwan yard to work with the horses, and apart from helping his father, Paddy never went to another trainer for experience. He learned his craft by making mistakes and by learning from those mistakes and by observation. He was also, of course, able to imbibe the knowledge of horses that came down in his family through the generations. Paddy says today, 'Going to another trainer might have been a help but it does tend to keep you from looking to do your own thing. You might just model yourself on him.' The big Irish trainers in Paddy's early years in the business were men like Paddy Sleator and Tom Dreaper. Paddy would try to figure out what they were doing that made them so successful. In the end, he never found out. All he could do was to slog away and to persevere, and he reckons that perseverance is one of the keys to success as a racehorse trainer. His early years were difficult enough and the rewards were few. As he says himself, 'It wasn't a very easy passage.' But the ability to persevere and never give up saw him through.

Paddy's first ride on a racecourse was at Naas, in a hunter's 'chase, in 1941, and there were no fewer than 31 runners. He didn't win and has a very hazy recollection today of what happened during the race but he does know that he finished the course. As was normal during the Second World War, or The Emergency as it was known in neutral Ireland, the horse he rode that day had to be brought to Naas by rail and then walked to the racecourse. The war had disrupted petrol supplies and only 'essential' motor trips were allowed by law. The powers-that-be did not regard getting a horse to a racecourse as an 'essential' trip. Recalls Paddy, 'The passenger trains would stick on a horse box at the tail end and away you went.' He would cycle from Doninga, leading the horse and proceed in this manner to the railway station at Bagenalstown or Gowran, for the onward rail journey to whatever station was nearest to the racecourse he wanted to reach.

While The Emergency caused particular problems as regards long-distance transport for horses, Paddy Mullins was used to roughing it when it came to getting a horse to its destination for a point-to-point. Although there was a certain amount of motor transport available before the war, it was only wealthy landowners who would have trailers or horse boxes. People taking horses to a race meeting would use a lorry, usually a hired lorry, and improvise with a tarpaulin thrown over the back. Of course, even this rough-and-ready method was disrupted during the war. Very often, rail transport was not used either. Frequently, a horse would be 'walked' to the meeting, led by a man in a pony and trap or on a bicycle and this was usually the case with point-to-points. Paddy Mullins recalls how he often 'walked' horses 15 miles behind a pony and trap to the Carlow Hunt point-to-point at Kellistown. He recalls, too, how the trainer John Kirwan would bring horses in similar fashion to the Coolattin Hunt's point-to-point at Shillelagh, Co. Wicklow – a distance of about 30 miles. 'He would run the horses, and win, and come home the same day, no bother.'

Travelling by rail with a horse during the war years could be a nightmare. Says Paddy, 'During the height of the Emergency, you never knew when the train was going to come. She could be stopped ten miles up the track for want of fuel. I remember on one occasion it took us from 1 o'clock in the day to about 3 o'clock in the morning to get from Gowran station to Tramore, a journey you would do now by car in half an hour. I don't know how many times the train had to be stopped to get up steam again. Travelling to Tramore there would be four horses in the one box car, each with a lad, with no partition between the horses and it was pitch dark – we could not see out. When we arrived in Waterford we would lead the horses across the city to the Tramore line, or ride them if they were quiet.'

Taking a horse from Doninga to Dundalk racecourse, a journey that these days would take less than three hours by road, was a major operation during the war years. Paddy remembers travelling with a horse by rail from Bagenalstown to Dublin the day before a race. Then he led the horse from Kingsbridge station to a nearby stables, Magee's yard in Montpelier Hill, where the animal was bedded down for the night. He himself stayed in nearby Ross's Hotel. Next day, Paddy took the horse by train via a circular route from Kingsbridge station to Amiens Street station, where the two of them, man and beast, embarked on the train to Dundalk. Another jockey was listed to ride. Arriving back in Amiens Street that night, Paddy led the horse through the busy city centre area of Dublin, past O'Connell Bridge and along by the banks of the Liffey to Kingsbridge Station, a distance of well over a mile. Then they caught the train for home. And after all that trouble, the horse, the inappropriately named Mighty Atom, didn't even win.

For those who have not lived through that era, it is difficult to imagine a racehorse, either a no-hoper or a star like the Dawn Run of a later era, being walked through the bustling downtown area of Dublin city in that way – especially by night.

Paddy remarks simply, 'We never minded these things – I don't know if it was because we were young. You would not lead a horse across the city now, with the traffic. All the people in those days were sympathetic towards horses but the drivers nowadays wouldn't have a clue. There was not the slightest bit of trouble from young lads in those days as you led a horse across the city. Times have certainly changed.'

Social life during the war years also frequently depended on horses. When cars went off the road as a result of wartime petrol restrictions, young people would resort to travelling great distances to dances by bicycle – or by pony and trap. As a bachelor, and before he began going out with his future wife Maureen, Paddy and his friends would go to dances. He recalls driving a pony and trap the 13 miles to a Red Cross dance in Kilkenny, taking a few friends with him. He says, 'To get to Kilkenny would take about an hour – a good trotting pony would do it in that time. In all the towns in those days there were yards where you could leave a pony – yards that were there for that purpose. You would come back to the yard, harness and yoke up your pony and head home in the darkness. You would have a light on the trap – a candle in a carriage lamp.'

The war years also saw a rare excursion by Paddy Mullins's father Willie into the world of politics. He was persuaded to stand in a general election for the Fine Gael party. The Mullins family were 'Free State' supporters – they backed those who had formed a government in Dublin following the Treaty with the British at the end of the War of Independence. This Free State government had then fought a civil war in the early 1920s with the Republicans who did not accept the terms of the Treaty with Britain. In the childhood of Paddy Mullins, in the wake of the civil war, constitutional politics had largely crystallised into two main blocs – those who supported the Free State policies of W. T. Cosgrave's Fine Gael party and those who supported the more 'Republican' or nationalist policies of Fianna Fáil and its leader Eamon de Valera. Says Paddy, 'In my young days, there were the Dev men and the Cosgrave men. That's largely how the country was divided. In a rural area like ours, everybody would know everybody else's politics. My own family were Cosgrave supporters. But we never took a great interest in active politics. However, my father was roped in to stand for Fine Gael in the general election of 1943, merely so he could pick up votes that would otherwise have been a help to Fianna Fail. Of course he never got elected. The reason he allowed his name to go forward is that he was a local man and it was thought he would get the local vote. It was silly, really.'

It would be hard to imagine the rather laconic and retiring Paddy Mullins handing out leaflets or canvassing for a political candidate, even if the candidate did happen to be his father. So what did he actually do during the election? Says Paddy, 'I didn't give out leaflets, nor did I canvass. My father didn't expect me to do anything nor did he ask me to do anything. In fact, I did absolutely nothing. Politics didn't come into my sphere at all. It was the same with all the family except my father and I think he just went with the tide when he was asked to stand. I had nothing whatever to do with it. Nothing whatever.'

CHAPTER 2

Modest Beginnings

Paddy Mullins will long remember a horse called Some Chicken. It had an extremely bad reputation for falling at fences and for throwing riders. But the Doninga man was to discover the horse's great hidden talent – and Some Chicken was to give Paddy his first ever win on a racecourse. And it was that happy experience that helped to give him the confidence to carry on, the confidence that he might just one day make it as a trainer. In the 1940s, Some Chicken was one of the most successful horses to be trained and ridden by Paddy, the training being carried out under the licence of John Kirwan. The horse belonged to Paddy Healy, who lived some miles from Doninga at Paulstown Castle. Healy was a very keen hunting man but as his own horse had been injured he was without a hunter. His close friend Major Dermot McCalmont of Mount Juliet made Healy a present of one of his own hunters, Some Chicken. The four-year-old horse was notorious for giving bad falls to riders and had already put two of McCalmont's men in hospital. It had never been ridden in a race.

Paddy Mullins recalls, 'Somebody made the remark, "What has Major McCalmont got against Paddy Healy that he would give him that horse!" Anyway, Paddy Healy got the horse and got his few falls off it. He gave it to me to hunt one day and although he didn't fall, he nearly fell so many times that I lost count. He was entered for the members' point-to-point at Doninga that year. I was training him for Paddy Healy for the race and to cut a long story short, he won in a canter, because racing was his game, not hunting. He was a terrific jumper at a fast pace but he could just not jump at a slow pace. It was funny that day. Major McCalmont was judge at the point-to-point and he happened to see me going out and he said, "Well, Mullins, what are you riding?". I said, "Some Chicken." "Oh," he says, "I'll say goodbye to you now because I won't be seeing you later!" This was 1943 and this was one of my most memorable wins. Here was a horse that was cast out by everybody and he turned out to be a marvellous racehorse.'

Later that year, Paddy was to have his first win as a rider on a racecourse, when Some Chicken won a bumper at Tramore. Paddy Healy shortly afterwards sold the horse to a publican who, in turn, sold him on to an owner in England. Some Chicken was to run in the Aintree Grand National, a testament to the way he impressed his connections in the UK. Paddy still has fond memories of the horse. It was the best he had handled up to then and riding him to victory on a racecourse helped to boost the confidence of the budding young jockey and trainer, who was still only in his early twenties.

Paddy's mainstay during this period was his work in the mundane world of hunters and point-to-pointers. As he says himself, 'After Some Chicken, good horses were few and far between for a few years. It was hard work, and there were some very nice people who asked me to take a horse now and then, and they were a big help. But at all times, and make no mistake, every young trainer finds the same thing – if a good horse or a promising horse appeared in my yard, there were always the people who would say, as they do at the present time, "If some other trainer had that horse, just imagine the results he would get." Every young trainer who gets a good horse finds himself the target of such comments. Then you have to have an owner who's rock steady, who will leave the horse with you.'

Paddy's father took out a licence to train in 1947. Paddy acted as an assistant or 'head man' to his father and in 1953 after being involved in training for 13 years, he took over the licence, his father making it clear that he himself did not wish to carry on. It was to prove a memorable year for Paddy. Earlier in 1953 before he took over the licence, Paddy rode a horse called Flash Parade II to victory in quite a prestigious race, the T. Levins-Moore Memorial Cup at Fairyhouse. The money he made from the win helped him shortly afterwards to buy his first car. On hand to see Paddy's moment of glory at Fairyhouse was his proud girlfriend, Maureen Doran, later to be his wife. After the race, Paddy celebrated in style. He took Maureen that evening for dinner to one of Dublin's most fashionable restaurants, The Bailey. Maureen came from Kilcruit, an area of Co. Carlow just across the river from Doninga, where her family had a big farm. She was a keen horsewoman and rode with the Mount Loftus Harriers. Like Paddy's three sisters, Maureen had attended the Brigidine convent school in Goresbridge, like their mothers and grandmothers before them. (In later years, Maureen's daughter Sandra would also attend the school for the earlier part of her education, establishing a family link across four generations with the convent.) At school, Maureen had become particularly friendly with Paddy's sister Evelyn and soon the friendship extended to Paddy himself and a romance developed.

The *Irish Field* commented thus on Paddy's win at Fairyhouse, 'There was a great finish to the T. Levins-Moore Memorial Plate, the Co. Kilkenny amateur Mr P. Mullins riding a magnificent race on Flash Parade II to win by a short head from the favourite, John Gorman, the mount of Mr M. F. Fogarty. John Gorman looked a winner as he cleared the last fence in front, but the strong riding of Mr Mullins on Flash Parade II gained the spoils for the six-year-old.' Later that year, on 29 April, Flash Parade II gave Paddy Mullins another reason to celebrate – the horse gave the Doninga man his first win as a trainer. It was during the Punchestown Festival and Paddy had just received his licence. The race was the La Touche Memorial Chase and Paddy was also the rider. The *Irish Field* once more paid tribute to the young rider-trainer. The journal hailed Paddy's performance in the gruelling 'chase thus, 'Best finish in the two days of truly memorable racing at the Punchestown Festival was that for the La Touche Cup, for which there were 19 runners facing the starter. At the end of this severe four and a half mile race, decided over the "old National Hunt" course, only a neck divided the winner, Flash Parade II from the dead-heaters, Left Alone and Grizzle. Near home, Mr P. Mullins put in some admirably strong work to land Flash Parade II as a winner.' Paddy had another winner that year, when Dress Parade won the Garryowen Handicap Hurdle at Limerick Junction.

In November 1954, Paddy and Maureen were married in St Mary's Church at Haddington Road, Dublin. The best man was Paddy's brother Luke, and the ushers were Tom Doran, a brother of the bride's, and Liam McGonagle, a second cousin of Paddy's and destined to become a leading Dublin solicitor. The bridesmaids were Maureen's sisters Peggy, Betty and Eileen. The reason the wedding was in Dublin was that Maureen had been working as a secretary in the city for the previous three years. Paddy would be leaving the family farm and would have to embark on making his own living. By the custom of the time, the large farm surrounding Doninga House had been earmarked for the eldest brother in the family, Jim. The other brothers would all have to carve out their own careers. Two of them, Bill (always known as Liam within the family) and Luke, who had both been educated at a boarding school, Knockbeg College in Co. Carlow, joined the Irish Army. However, for Paddy, there was only one career – a career with horses. It was what he always wanted but, at the same time, he felt he did not have much choice, since there was no way he would be inheriting the farm at Doninga House.

Bill and Luke both retained their love of horses while pursuing careers as army officers. Bill, who became an officer after graduating from the cadet school, went on to become a noted member of the Irish Army showjumping team that was re-formed after the Second World War. His great moment of glory was at the Royal Dublin Society Horse Show in 1949. The Irish won the prestigious Aga Khan Cup at the RDS, with Bill, riding Bruree, having the best individual round. (Bill's son Brian would, in later years, ride in races for Paddy.) Bill was Quartermaster General of the army when he retired – one of the highest ranks in the force. Luke became an officer after joining the army during The Emergency as a private. After he retired from the army Luke was, for many years, the manager of Galway racecourse. His son David has a stud farm in Kentucky. Of the three sisters in the family, Evelyn, or Evie as she was known, maintained the military connection by marrying an army officer, Philip Eager, now retired. They live at Newbridge, Co. Kildare. Mary is married and living near Athy, and Ursula is married and living in Wexford. Paddy's eldest brother Jim, as well as running the farm at Doninga, was also to become chairman of a leading company in the meat business, Cork Marts. A fine point-to-point rider, he died from a heart attack in 1980, the day after attending a St Stephen's Day hunt. Doninga House, the old family residence, is now occupied by Jim's widow Mary, her son Gerard and his wife. Another son Seamus is a trainer in England.

Paddy was 35 and Maureen was more than 10 years younger when they tied the knot. 'I waited for her,' he grins. The couple spent their honeymoon in Paris, in a hotel that somebody arranged for them on the rue d'Alger, in an area off the fashionable rue de Rivoli on the Right Bank. It was an upmarket area, but despite this the living was easy in the Paris of those years and everything was very cheap. Paddy, who never lost the soft accent of south Leinster, was given a crash course in French pronunciation on his first trip to Paris. A taxi driver professed not to understand when Paddy asked to be taken to the rue d'Alger. All was clarified when Paddy wrote out the name of the street on a piece of paper. The cabbie proceeded to tell the man from Goresbridge how the words should be pronounced in French. The newly-weds saw the usual sights, the Eiffel Tower, the Mona Lisa, the Champs-Elysées, but the highlight of the trip was the races at Auteuil. More than 40 years on, Maureen still has the race card for their day out at Auteuil, the premier French jump track. It was to be Paddy's first taste of racing in Paris and he cast a keen professional's eye over the way the French racing people operated. He thought he would love to have a runner there some time but little did he realise that he would one day enjoy his own moments of spectacular glory on the race track in Paris.

In the meantime, Paddy worked very hard to get his training career under way. The newly-weds moved into a house at Doninga, about a half mile from the old family residence. Paddy's new abode was an old two-storey farmhouse. It had once been the home of the steward of the Doninga House estate, and had a certain elegance about it, a certain period charm. Paddy rented at first from the owners, people called Crampton, and later bought the property. The long house with its large Georgian windows and the creepers clinging to the white walls, has a secluded garden enclosed by high hedges and is still the home of Paddy and Maureen Mullins to this day. When Paddy moved in first, there were just a couple of acres attached to the house, but he gradually built up his land holding and he would be still building on boxes into the 1980s.

The years from 1954 to 1960 he describes as his 'building period'. 'They were the years when I was feeling my way as a trainer.' He fixed up three or four boxes at his new home when he moved in and they were mostly used for horses that were being broken. He was fortunate that he also had the use of the stables at the old family house and horses that were running were kept there. He was mostly concentrating on point-to-point horses for about four years from 1954 and he did not have many winners under Rules during that period – only five. In better times in later decades he could notch up that number easily in a few days.

One of Paddy's better horses around the time he married was Crosspatrick. Indeed this horse was to give the newly-weds a very pleasing wedding present – a win at Naas just after they returned from their honeymoon. Maureen recalls that Paddy knew the horse didn't need much work, and just asked the lad at home to walk him while they were away in Paris. In December 1954 Crosspatrick rewarded Paddy's confidence in him when, with Paddy in the saddle, he won a bumper at Naas, the Paulstown Plate, the prize money being 100 sovereigns. Earlier in 1954, Paddy had won a Kilkenny Hunt point-to-point with the horse. Paddy's only other winner that year was Errand Boy, who won the Dowdall Hall Handicap Chase at Dundalk. The owner of Crosspatrick was Tom Nicholson whose horse Vulpine, trained by Paddy, was later to win the Irish Grand National. Tom Nicholson came from a family with a big farm at Johnstown, Co. Kilkenny and had a keen interest in horses. He hunted and rode in North Kilkenny Hunt point-to-points. He bought Crosspatrick as a three-year-old, named after a neighbouring village, for the then unheard of sum of £300, and became one of Paddy's earliest owners as the Doninga man began training under his own name.

Crosspatrick was later to be sold to England for ten times what Nicholson paid for him, for the then fabulous price of £3,000. 'That was money in those days,' says Paddy. The horse was bought by the noted English trainer Peter Cazalet, who trained for the Queen Mother. Cazalet sent two Irish experts to see the horse at Doninga before purchase. These were Judge W. E. Wylie, who had become first chairman of the Racing Board in the 1940s, and who also became a Steward of the Turf Club, and a leading horse dealer, David Harvey, whom Paddy regards as one of the best judges of a horse in the country at that period. Paddy recalls that he and Maureen had just moved into the house at the time. Even though one of the first things they did on moving in was to apply for a phone, it still had not been installed.

So the two emissaries of the Queen Mother's trainer had to make their way to the little post office in Goresbridge about two miles away. This happens to be the oldest post office in Europe, dating back to 1845, and run by the Moffatt family for the past five generations. From there, the two men phoned Cazalet on a crackling line to say that the horse was fine and that the deal could go ahead. Cazalet was, of course, the trainer of the Queen Mother's horse, Devon Loch who was at the centre of a sensation in the 1956 Aintree Grand National. The horse, ridden by Dick Francis who was later to become a noted thriller writer, was in the lead and looked absolutely certain to win when it suddenly collapsed within 50 yards of the finishing line. Recalls Paddy, 'Tom Nicholson took Maureen and myself over to Lingfield to see Crosspatrick in his first race in England. Dick Francis was the jockey and I spoke to him before the horse went out, and I remember telling him what kind of horse he was. Crosspatrick was not able to win although well-fancied. He probably was taking on a better class than he had been used to in Ireland.' Paddy and Maureen Mullins still see Dick Francis almost every year at Cheltenham, and Paddy has become a fan of Francis's racing thrillers. Says Paddy, 'The racing background in the books is absolutely authentic.'

January 1955 marked the end of an era in the history of Doninga House, the old Mullins homestead. The Mount Loftus Harriers held their last point-to-point ever that month and it was run, as usual, over the Mullins farm and neighbouring farms. Maureen had ridden with the local hunt but she had never taken part in a race and had an all-consuming ambition to do so. Thus it came about that the newly-weds competed against each other in the last point-to-point at Doninga, with Paddy riding a horse called Blunt Lady. Maureen was pregnant at the time with her first child, Sandra.

'It was madness when you look back on it,' says Paddy now. 'Maureen achieved her ambition anyway, but she didn't finish the race. I looked back to see if she was there and she wasn't. I think the mare she was riding, Mulatto, took over half way and brought her home!' Says Maureen, 'It was so different from the point-to-points today. I will never forget it. You had these very difficult drop banks, about five of them after starting. The point-to-points of that time were quite dangerous. I was out of my mind to do it. The speed we were going at! In the end I pulled up.' Perhaps it was appropriate that the winner of the last point-to-point at Doninga House that day was Paddy Mullins himself.

The 1955 to 1958 period was a lean one for the stable, with three winners in 1956, two in 1957 and blank years in 1955 and 1958. All five wins came from Paddy's own horse, Fortlass, who won bumpers at Tramore in May 1956 and Kilbeggan the following August. Fortlass followed that with a win in a handicap hurdle at Thurles in November of that year. In 1957 Fortlass registered the two wins in handicap hurdles, the first at Kilbeggan in August and then in Leopardstown in November. It was Paddy's first win as a trainer in Leopardstown and few present on the day could have foreseen that the little-known trainer from Goresbridge would later experience such moments of glory on the same track.

'It was not an easy time, looking back on it now,' says Paddy. 'It certainly was a learning process. I learned that no matter how well you think your horses are in shape, there are times when you just draw a blank. This happens to even the biggest stables. Sometimes, unaccountably, the winners just dry up and then, just as quickly and for no apparent reason, the stable starts to turn out winners again. But you just have to keep going, day after day. I was lucky at the time, that I had other ways of making money, such as breaking horses and training them for point-to-points. Otherwise I might not have been able to carry on.'

There was a vast improvement in Paddy's fortunes in 1959 when he registered nine winners – almost double the total for the previous four years. By now he had acquired a very valued client, Tony Onions, who was to be with him for many years. In 1959 Onions rode his own horse Gallant Barney to success in two bumpers at Navan, one in February and the other in April. Tom Nicholson's Lady Artist II also had a win, while a horse owned by his brother Alfie, Whatever, won four races. Whatever was piloted to two bumper wins, at Galway in July and at Mallow in September, by Francis Flood. John Conway took the same mount for hurdle wins at Clonmel in November and Limerick in December.

Paddy also rode Whatever during that same year, 1959, and it was to prove a highly significant occasion for the rider from a personal point of view. It was to be his last ride on a racecourse. He had been riding in races, both point-to-points and under Rules, all during the 1950s. But the end of his riding career came when he took a very bad fall off Whatever at Limerick Junction in November. The result of the fall was that he suffered a cracked vertebra and spent six weeks in hospital, on a hard bed. He came home with plaster all over him and had to wear a brace on his back for a couple of months afterwards. He reckons he was out of action for almost a year. The injury persuaded him to give up his riding career and to concentrate on training.

'I knew after that fall that my riding days were over,' he says. 'Besides, at that stage, the horses needed all my attention and there were plenty of good jockeys out there whom I could engage.' Paddy Mullins has always been one to spot early talent not only in a horse but also in a young jockey. Observing new jockeys at work is something he does when he goes to a race meeting. In more recent times the advent of races on video has enabled him to study in more detail the style of young riders coming up in the business – a kind of talent-spotting. Even during those early lean years, Paddy had some of the best riders on his horses. Francis Flood, a gifted amateur and now a very successful trainer, rode for Paddy on many occasions, as did G. W. Robinson and Kevin Prendergast. Kevin had just returned from Australia and was assistant to his renowned father, P. J. 'Darkie' Prendergast who was not at all pleased to see him riding for the Goresbridge trainer. Said Paddy, 'P. J. obviously did not want to see Kevin in any danger, and gave him some stick for taking mounts for me. Kevin went on to follow in his father's footsteps as a trainer and I am delighted to see he is still turning out regular winners.'

Around the beginning of the 1960s, Paddy Mullins began gradually to move away from training point-to-point horses as better horses came into his yard. The long years of hard work – he had been involved in training for at least 20 years – began to pay off at this period. His reputation was growing and owners began to send good horses to him. Sometimes a satisfied owner would introduce another owner to him, and Paddy would thus acquire another client.

It was well for Paddy that at last he began making the breakthrough – his family was growing steadily. Sandra was born in October 1955, followed by William in September the following year. Then there was George (October 1959); Tony (January 1962) and Tom (May 1964). Paddy's father Willie died in 1963 – late enough to get to know his several grandchildren, and to see his son making a success of his training career. Paddy's mother had died from cancer in 1954 at the quite young age of 63.

People sometimes remark to Paddy how hard things must have been for him, starting off as a little-known trainer. But while he recognises that it was a struggle to get going, he never himself, at the time, thought of life being hard. He and Maureen were just too busy raising their children and building up the business. Besides, he was working at something he really enjoyed, something to which he was absolutely dedicated. It wasn't just a job – it was a vocation, a way of life. He admits that, at first, it was not an easy decision to become a trainer. He was staking his career and the future of his family on being successful. He remarks now, 'I always had it at the back of my mind that if I didn't make it I would go off and get a job somewhere. If things had not worked out I would have headed to America. I would have looked for a job in racing or on a stud farm. I often think I would have done better if I had gone to America. I often regret it. I nearly did go once, after we were married. We had only one or two children at the time. I wonder what might have happened had I gone to America. I see fellows out there at the present time, I happen to meet them when I go out there, and I know damn well some of them haven't half the experience that I have, and they are doing really well, and I have the regrets then. But going to America would have meant uprooting everything . . . '

Paddy got some of his first really good horses in the early 1960s after the Kirwan stables, just a few miles from Doninga, closed down. John Kirwan, Paddy's old mentor, had died and the stables were taken over by John's son Dan who himself died in 1960 at the early age of 48. This sad event was to prove very significant for Paddy, because with the closure of the Kirwan stables, owners began to look elsewhere for a trainer to take charge of their horses. A number of former Kirwan patrons decided to send their horses to Paddy Mullins and, as Paddy says, 'My first really decent animals came onstream.'

One of those first really decent animals was a mare by Artist's Son called Height O'Fashion, one of a number of successful horses owned by an auctioneer and valuer from Goresbridge, Jack Donohoe. Years before, Paddy had won a race with Height O'Fashion's mother, Dress Parade. Among the other Donohoe horses that came to Doninga were Errand Boy and Fashion's Fancy. But the one that was to prove the real star among them was Height O'Fashion. She ran at three but not successfully. In early 1961, at age four, she won her first race, a bumper at Thurles, the Corinthian Plate, ridden by Frank Lacy who had family connections with the owner. 'She was a really good one,' says Paddy. 'She went on to win five more races that year, and another six the following year, making it 12 wins in all.'

The mare, who had shown her ability over hurdles and fences, kept the best wine until last by winning the 1962 Irish Cesarewitch at The Curragh. Carrying only 7st 5lb, and ridden by John Wright, she won easily at 7–1 from the 7–2 favourite De Reski. Later that year the mare came third in the November Handicap at Leopardstown. In winning the Cesarewitch, Height O'Fashion had given Paddy his biggest win to date. The mare also played an unwitting role in improving the feed of the horses at the Doninga stables. Paddy attributes much of his success, from this period on, to the diet that he introduced for his horses. He says, 'I would say that the biggest factor in my success, if you can call it that, was the feeding of the horses. We went over to a balanced ration when nobody was doing it, with the help of Liam Connolly, the local food provender, who ran the Red Mills company. The same Height O'Fashion was instrumental in it.

'We brought her to Newcastle to run in a big sponsored hurdle there in 1962. She did not win, and on the way back they were held up in Holyhead for over two weeks because they could not ship the horses with the heavy seas. When the lad with the mare, Martin Carroll, finally got home, I asked him how did they manage as regards food. "Oh," he said, "they brought us nuts." Well, we had no experience of horse nuts. I don't know if we had even heard of them at the time. The horse loved them. Martin had a few of the nuts with him when he came home and I said to myself, "Why couldn't we have nuts for our horses as well?"'

Paddy had a meeting with Liam Connolly at the Red Mills plant in Goresbridge. The two men knew each other from school. Recalls Paddy, 'I asked Liam if he could make up a balanced ration for horses in a nut form. He called in a very good animal dietitian, a Wicklow man called Jim Ryan, and he made out a ratio for the ingredients. It was in meal form then, because it was before Liam installed a cubing facility to make the nuts, and we started feeding it. We fed the meal as an addition to oats and gradually we worked our way into the nuts, and they were improved as time went on, and our horses started to come forward.

'You can rest assured that this was what lifted me out of the depths in the 1960s and on into the 1970s. I remember the time we went to America with one of our best horses ever, Herring Gull, to race him in Camden in South Carolina in 1970. We got a chance to go up to Lexington, Kentucky and to visit a few studs and stables and I saw them feeding these nuts. I got Liam Connolly to make up nuts specially for us based on the nuts we found in America. It was a complete success, to the degree that it got about naturally with our lads in the yard that we were getting a different nut from Connolly. People were all looking for Paddy Mullins's nuts! Liam Connolly made a great success of Red Mills horse nuts and it is a flourishing business to this day.'

If Height O'Fashion played a role in the introduction of an important new feeding regime for Paddy Mullins's horses, the animal also played a role in a major crisis for the stable. A disagreement arose in 1963 between Paddy and the owner of

Height O'Fashion, Jack Donohoe, which resulted in Paddy asking Mr Donohoe to remove his horses from the yard. For a trainer to turn away a major client was regarded by some at the time as the height of lunacy, and there were those who doubted if the Mullins yard would survive. Paddy recalls, 'The winter of 1962/63 had been very severe. There was a month of icy, frozen conditions. The horses had not been getting work. Then when the weather broke, we started to work them, but the animals were not fit enough.

'Height O'Fashion ran what Mr Donohoe regarded as a below par race in her first outing in 1963, in the Thyestes Chase at Gowran Park. It was due to the amount of fat the horse was carrying – she was out of condition. Mr Donohoe let me know his feelings in no uncertain terms. I felt he did not appreciate the problems involved. In fact, Height O'Fashion became a better mare because of the lay-off. But I felt that Mr Donohoe was taking advice from a lot of other people instead of listening to me. That was the basis of our difference of opinion. So I asked him to take his horses away. People thought that he took the initiative in taking them away, but this is not the case. The trainer Joe Osborne took Height O'Fashion and a couple of other young horses that were very promising went to another trainer, Tom Lacy. It was freely said at the time that Paddy Mullins is finished now. But we survived.'

Height O'Fashion went on to take part in some memorable struggles with the renowned Arkle, on one occasion running him to a neck when receiving three stone of weight. She also came second to Arkle in the Irish Grand National. Paddy says he had always been friends with Mr Donohoe and they were reconciled after their disagreement. He said he would always have to remember that Mr Donohoe had given him his horses in the first place and that they had been a huge help to the yard in the early years. The disagreement with Jack Donohoe underlines a basic element in Paddy's philosophy as a trainer. The Doninga man takes an immense pride in his work and for him the most important requirement for an owner is that he should appreciate the work done by the stable.

Although he is as eager as the next man to be paid by his clients, and although getting paid is a constant headache for many trainers, Paddy still considers the 'appreciation' principle to be paramount, transcending even the question of money. Back in the 1960s he was even prepared to put a severe dent in his income for the sake of that principle when he turned away the Donohoe horses. He has no doubt mellowed since then and nowadays would not be as inclined to take such drastic action. But the principle of 'appreciation' remains very important to him. 'If an owner shows appreciation, you can put up with a lot,' he says.

Of course, when it comes to removing horses from a trainer's yard, the system can work both ways. Many a trainer has been shocked to find that an owner has decided on his own initiative, that his horse, or horses, for whatever reason, are to be taken away and sent to another yard. Says Paddy, 'It happens all the time that owners move their horses around from stable to stable. Happily, it has rarely happened to me. But it does frequently occur, and owners don't have to give you any reason for taking a horse away. They are free to do it, as long as their bill is paid up. I always say that between a trainer and an owner the bottom line is this – the owner can say to the trainer, "I'll take my horses away" or the trainer can say to the owner, "You take your horses away". All the rest is only talk. The bottom line is that. And I always keep it in my mind. The idea of signing a contract with an owner to train his horse, say, for a couple of years, I don't think that would work. I wouldn't be a party to it anyway. I would leave it the way it is. A contract would not be feasible because there are too many unforeseen things that can happen to horses. If you needed a contract to keep somebody in the yard, it would be a very poor relationship, and you would be better off out of it.'

CHAPTER 3

Making Headway

Turning away some of the best horses in his yard was an extremely risky thing to do for Paddy Mullins as he tried to get his training career under way. It could be said that this trainer who never gambled heavily and was too superstitious to even back his own horses, had taken a huge gamble with his own future. But somehow Maureen knew that things would work out. She knew that Paddy had all the ability and talent and knowledge that he needed as a trainer and had proven it with his handling of Height O'Fashion. She felt that people would recognise his competence and would send their horses to him. Everything worked out more or less as she had anticipated.

Shortly after the departure of the Donohoe horses, a great window of opportunity opened up for Paddy Mullins. It so happened that a leading trainer at the time, Colonel A. J. Blake from Co. Laois, had decided to retire. Colonel Blake, who was based at the The Heath House, Maryborough had a lot of high society clients. Says Paddy, 'He was the crème de la crème. Anybody who was anybody would want to have a horse with him.' The colonel had, many years before, succeeded his uncle, a renowned racing figure from the nineteenth century, C. J. Blake, as head of the Maryborough stables. One of the colonel's biggest and most valued clients was a major landowner, Robert Hall-Dare, who had an estate at Newtownbarry, near Bunclody, Co. Wexford. And after Colonel Blake closed down, Mr Hall-Dare asked Paddy if he would take three or four horses. We don't have to guess at Paddy's reply and the horses came to Doninga in 1963.

The arrival of the Hall-Dare horses marked a serious move by Paddy into Flat racing – and it was also to mark the beginning of an extremely happy business relationship. Paddy recalls, 'Mr Hall-Dare was a great client, and he stayed with me until he died. He was a lovely man, a great man to have any association with. He was a Flat man. He had the odd jumper but he bred for the Flat and raced on the Flat. The Hall-Dare horses were very well bred but they had not had very much success. Somehow they started winning races after coming to me. Mr Hall-Dare had a tremendous interest in horses. He was a great hunting man and hunted with the Island Hounds for many years. For ten years we had a tremendous association, and we even went to France with a very good horse of his, Nor, and won a race at Maisons-Laffitte.'

It was unusual at the time for an Irish trainer to go to France, but according to Paddy, Bobby Hall-Dare was always ready to do something new or unusual. Nor was even sent to Germany to take part in a race but without success. Nor had a great moment of glory when it notched up a fourth to the great Nijinsky in the Irish Sweeps Derby in 1970. Says Paddy, 'Mr Hall-Dare was a man who never spent money on himself. He may have been involved in the social scene when he was younger but later he lived a very quiet life. Everything was for the horses. He was a great man for travelling if he had anything to travel with. He would love to go to Ascot or anywhere like that and to France as well. Nothing seemed to worry him. He would never say die. The one thing you were not to say to him was that his horse disappointed. He would be consoling me if his horse had not done well. Colonel Blake was heard to remark once that the really good clients he had in his day were Bobby Hall-Dare and the President of Ireland. I would say he was referring to how they paid.'

Mr Hall-Dare's daughter Clody, now Mrs Norton, presently runs a stud farm in Bunclody, Co. Wexford, and she recalls one episode that illustrates the ability of Paddy Mullins with her father's horses. 'There was a horse called Wild Impulse, a funny old character and he had been kept in the garden here at our house for most of the winter and had done nothing. Then he went back to Doninga and I think Paddy only had him for three weeks and then produced him in a race at the Phoenix Park, one of the first of the season and Wild Impulse proceeded to win. I remember him running away with the race. He was an outsider, nobody fancied him and we all had very small amounts of money on him and the odds were enormous. There was piles of money paid out on our small bets of £1 or so. However, my father never really gambled.' Bobby Hall-Dare died in 1972 when his horses were still at Doninga and doing well.

The arrival of horses from Mr Hall-Dare and other owners meant that from the 1960s onwards, Paddy Mullins had both Flat and National Hunt horses in his yard. As regards National Hunt, it is not generally known that, back in 1960, Paddy trained a horse which, shortly after leaving his stable, went on to win the Aintree Grand National. The horse in question was Nicolaus Silver and it was one of the horses that came to him as a result of the closure of the neighbouring Kirwan stable. The horse had been bred in Co. Tipperary by James Heffernan and had originally been owned by Joe Smithwick, a member of a prominent Kilkenny business family. On his death, the horse had been sold to two brothers called Hutchinson. Recalls Paddy, 'After Dan Kirwan died the horse came to me. He had been out on grass and was as fat as a pig. We put him in training and kept him going for several months. He was a lovely horse but we never got to run him. The owners decided to sell him and we took him to Goff's Sales in November 1960 and he was sold to the English trainer Fred Rimell, who bought him on behalf of a client. He made £2,600 and a well-known trainer, who shall remain nameless, was heard to remark with disdain that if you took a nought off that figure you would be closer to the real value of the horse.

'Fred Rimell began training Nicolaus Silver in England and, 16 weeks after he left our stable, he won the Aintree Grand National of 1961. He won by five lengths from Merryman II, the previous year's winner.' Up to that year Nicolaus Silver was only the second grey horse ever to win the Grand National, the other one being the Irish-bred horse, The Lamb, who won the race twice, in 1868 and 1871. Paddy himself was to have at least three runners in the Aintree Grand National over the years but without success. The horses were Luska, Dudie and The Gooser.

Paddy had his first entry at the Cheltenham Festival in 1962. In fact it was his first venture into racing outside Ireland. He entered a horse called Raining for a four mile amateur novice chase at the festival. The horse had been owned by the Mullins family and had been sold to a London businessman, the late Chris Akers, who was eager to have a runner at Cheltenham. Paddy recalls Raining as a 'big, slow horse'. Raining had won only once, in a novice chase at Gowran Park some months previously. Paddy recalls with a chuckle how he arrived at Cheltenham racecourse on the morning of the race. The horse's jockey on the day, Francis Flood, had been delayed and Paddy was anxious to school Raining over the course. Bobby Beasley had just given a run around the track to one of the horses of Paddy Sleator, one of the most prominent Irish National Hunt trainers at the time. Beasley said he would give Raining a 'spin' around the course. Raining was certainly not one of the fastest horses at the festival that year and Sleator and some of his friends watched Raining's ponderous progress around the track.

Paddy smiles as he recalls Sleator's characteristic West Wicklow drawl as the Grangecon trainer remarked loudly to his pals, 'That fella will go a long way – in a long time.' As it turned out, Francis Flood extracted a good performance from Raining in the race that afternoon, finishing a very creditable fifth. The fact that Paddy was one of the 'small' trainers in that era made it all the more gratifying whenever one of his horses had the good fortune to beat the horses of the 'big boys', with whom he would only have had a passing acquaintance at the time. Apart from Paddy Sleator, the big trainers at this period would have included Paddy Prendergast, Tom Dreaper, Vincent O'Brien and John Oxx.

Of the notable Flat jockeys he dealt with during the earlier part of his career, Paddy Mullins has an extremely high regard for Johnny Roe, an old friend who now lives in the Far East, and Buster Parnell. The jockey whom he rates as the best jump jockey of all time is Martin Molony, whose meteoric career was brought to an early close by a heavy fall at Thurles. Says Paddy, 'I remember Johnny Roe and Buster riding for me one season. They were competing for the championship at the time, and were vying for any rides they could get, including mine. They were both extremely good Flat jockeys. In my estimation, Martin Molony was the best jump jockey of all time. He was brilliant. He retired due to injury when he was only in his twenties, and so many people have never heard of him. All too often in this business you're forgotten once you drop out. Molony had the strength of two men and was not huge. He could ride a lazy horse from the beginning to the finish of a race and be fresh and strong at the end. One race stands out in my mind. He was riding a bad horse in a three mile chase and was no way entitled to win it. But Martin was off the bridle from the time they jumped off until they finished and by sheer ability he just brought him home to win. He is retired now and has a stud farm but doesn't train. He had a brother Tim, also a very good jockey.'

In 1964 the Mullins stable doubled the previous year's number of winners. Devenish Artist, owned by George Doran, a brother of Maureen's, recorded four successes during that year, and Indicate, owned by John Mernagh had four wins in the same period. On 8 August at Tramore, Burst Flush, owned by Jerry O'Neill recorded his first win, and was to have a total of eight over a three year period. Another horse who was to prove a real money-spinner for the stable, Mick McQuaid, had his first win at Leopardstown on 21 November, in the Farewell Nursery. The horse belonged to Mr Hall-Dare, having been bought as a yearling. 'Mick McQuaid was ridden at Leopardstown that day by a very small boy,' says Paddy. 'His name was Michael Hourigan, who is now one of the most successful trainers in the country.' Mick McQuaid went on to register eight more wins on the Flat and over hurdles in a three year period.

Around the time that Robert Hall-Dare sent horses to Paddy Mullins, another interesting owner also became a valued client – Mrs Doreen Archer Houblon. She lived on a country estate at Kilmurry, near Thomastown, Co. Kilkenny and was an accomplished rider. She had the unusual distinction of being one of the foremost experts in side-saddle techniques in Britain or Ireland. Every year she would go to London for a month to prepare Queen Elizabeth and her horse for the side-saddle riding required during the annual Trooping of the Colour ceremony. Mrs Archer Houblon sent horses to be trained with Paddy. One of the better ones was Solwezi, who came to Doninga as a foal to be trained as a two-year-old. Solwezi had been given to Mrs Archer Houblon by a friend in England, and the name was said to have been suggested by Queen Elizabeth after a place she had visited in Kenya.

Mrs Archer Houblon, in turn, introduced Paddy to another important owner, Lady Elizabeth Byng, who also sent horses to be trained at Doninga. Lady Elizabeth lived in Hertfordshire and at one stage had horses in training with Capt. Tim Forster. She was a close friend of Mrs Archer Houblon whom she would often visit at Kilmurry. They had worked together in a munitions factory in England during the Second World War. Lady Elizabeth, a daughter of the Earl of Stafford, used to keep horses with Mrs Archer Houblon, one of which, Painter's Cottage, was sent to the Mullins yard.

Painter's Cottage won point-to-point races and managed to give the Mullins stable a good start to the 1963 season by winning the Blackwater Hunter Chase at Mallow on 13 April, following this with a win in the valuable Tetratema Chase at Gowran Park on 16 May. Overall, the season was a quiet one for the Doninga stable. Paddy was only to produce four more winners that year to record six successes in all. Yet his reputation as a sound, reliable trainer was spreading slowly but surely. He was building up a solid base of good owners and good horses and he was learning all the time. Lady Elizabeth was to supply him with one of his better horses of the 1970s. This was Counsel Cottage, who was to win the Sun Alliance Hurdle at the Cheltenham Festival in 1977, ridden by Sean Treacy, an uncle of T. P. Treacy who currently rides for the Mullins stable.

For some odd reason, Paddy, as a trainer during this period, seemed to attract elderly genteel ladies as owners. One of the owners who stands out in his mind from this period is the late Mrs Mary Channing. She lived in the old rectory at Gowran with her husband, a retired RAF Wing Commander. He had lived in many exotic parts of the world and he had first met his wife in the Far East. Down through the years Mrs Channing had horses with various trainers, including Phonsie O'Brien.

Recalls Paddy, 'Mrs Channing was a lovable old lady who was mad about horses but had some weird ideas. She had a horse with the trainer Mickey Curran who told her once after an unsuccessful race that the distance didn't suit the horse – he needed a longer distance. She stored it in her mind and the next time in the parade ring she told the jockey to go around on the outside because the trainer had said the horse needed a longer trip. She also had a brood mare and it was always a hassle getting her in foal but this year she sent off the urine samples and the result came back negative. Mrs Channing just said casually that she knew the mare was in foal and that the experts had probably got the bottles mixed up. She turned out to be absolutely right about the mare – she was in foal.

'Mrs Channing had a horse with us called Touraine. It was one of the more successful horses she had. She would come to the races with us, sitting in the back of the car, chain-smoking Woodbines through an elegant cigarette holder. It was Woodbines all the way, nothing but Woodbines. You'd have to fumigate the car afterwards. Her husband had no interest in the horses. He would go to the pub in Gowran and his favourite drink was a pint of Smithwicks with a glass of gin mixed into it. He had a glass eye and told us how he lost it after it popped out in a plane once. Managed to find it too, after a long search. He used to tell us how he blundered into the grounds of a harem on his travels abroad. He said the oul' eunuchs went mad when they spotted him. He said he was never as lucky to get away as when the eunuchs chased after him.'

One of the better horses Paddy had in his stable during the 1960s was Mrs Archer Houblon's Solwezi. He recalls Solwezi as a very decent horse, one of his first good Flat horses. Solwezi won a maiden at Gowran Park on 4 June 1965, with Mick Kennedy riding. It was just one of the 26 winners that Paddy was to have that year, his highest tally of winners to date. Mrs Archer Houblon wanted to see Solwezi run in the Irish Derby so Paddy entered him for the big event at The Curragh, even though he had his reservations, considering that the one and a half mile distance did not suit him. Solwezi, partnered by G. W. Robinson, finished way down the field. The race was won that year by Meadow Court, ridden by Lester Piggott. Meadow Court was owned in part by the singer Bing Crosby, who was present on the day.

Solwezi won two more races that year but was unlucky in the Irish Cambridgeshire at The Curragh. In that race, ridden by Johnny Roe, Solwezi led up to the line only to be beaten by a neck by Courtwell, trained by the late Charlie Weld, father of the trainer Dermot Weld. Solwezi was later sold as a three-year-old to an owner in America but before he could ever run in a race there he met with an unfortunate accident. He took fright while out on the road, jumped into a ditch and was killed. Solfeggio was another horse owned by Mrs Archer Houblon, and she was to have three wins with Solfeggio in 1971.

Counsel Cottage, who was to give Paddy a memorable moment of glory at Cheltenham, was bred by Lady Elizabeth Byng herself. Recalls Paddy, 'Lady Elizabeth was a great old lady who had her own ideas about everything but who was not difficult by any stretch of the imagination. Since she had a mare who was going to stud she decided that she would buy a stallion nomination to Counsel, a Two Thousand Guineas winner at the time but who was starting to go downhill. And she decided that she would make all the arrangements herself. So she went along, on her own, to where they sell these nominations on a certain day and she bid and got her nomination to Counsel. The foal was Counsel Cottage, who was to prove a very good horse.

'Lady Elizabeth, who died a few years back at the age of 90, came to Galway once or twice to see her horses running. She was the most independent lady you could ever know. She was in her seventies at this stage. I remember in Galway she was heading for the train after the races – we had driven her down. She was carrying two heavy cases. I said, "Give me those cases now" and she refused point blank. I said "Give me one of them, anyway" and she said "No, no – they keep me balanced like this." And she was only a small woman. She was one of the real old stock.' Paddy reckons that after the departure of Jack Donohoe's horses, the owners who really gave his stable a boost were Robert Hall-Dare, Mrs Archer Houblon and Lady Elizabeth Byng. 'They really lifted me up.' Two of Mrs Archer Houblon's Thomastown neighbours also sent horses to Paddy during the 1960s. Colonel M. F. Palmer enjoyed success with his horse Newsletter while Major Desmond Lambert had a number of wins with his mare Black Outlook. The late Major Lambert lived in Dysart Moore, a house by the banks of the Nore that figures prominently in the 1995 film *Circle of Friends*, based on a Maeve Binchy novel.

In his early years, Paddy Mullins would charge a weekly rate of £3.10s (£3.50), later £4 for the upkeep and training of a horse. It seems like a modest amount nowadays, but there were times when it was difficult to get the fees from a minority of owners. He recalled one man who didn't pay for about two years. Apart from sending out his regular bills, Paddy never approached the man for the money but just kept on training the horse. It went against the grain to be haggling over money. Ultimately the owner paid his debts in full. The vast majority of owners he acquired over the years paid the agreed fees. But when he started training, there were no procedures whereby a trainer got a guaranteed percentage of the prize money. Recalls Paddy, 'The owner paid you what you struck with him as being the weekly upkeep of the horse. But there were no percentages to which a trainer was entitled as of right. There were owners who would not dream of giving anything after a win. If the horse won a big prize, some owners would give you a present, others would give you a token amount and others would give you nothing.

'It was in the late 1960s that the Turf Club introduced the percentage system for trainers, and they deducted the money at source from the prize money. It's something that had often been sought by the trainers. Before the Turf Club rule came in, my own owners, like Mr Hall-Dare, had agreed voluntarily to have the Turf Club deduct the percentage earmarked for the stable from the prize money. There was just one exception – one man said he would only have the percentage deducted from "win" money, not "place money"! When the whole thing was formalised, we were getting 10 per cent at first from the Turf Club and then they deducted 2 per cent from it to fund pension schemes for people working in the industry.'

By the mid-1960s, Paddy Mullins had established a secure reputation as a trainer in both Flat and in National Hunt racing. In a book published by Pelham Books in 1967, *The Horse in Ireland* by Noel Phillips Browne, he is listed among the 'modern Irish trainers of distinction'. The book refers to him as 'a Kilkenny farmer-turned-trainer, whose placing in the trainers' list improves each season'. At this period, horses from the Mullins stable were really making their presence felt, especially on the National Hunt scene. Although falling short of the previous year's total of 26 winners, 1966 saw the introduction of what was to be Paddy's first Irish Grand National winner, Vulpine. The horse had wins at Gowran Park, Fairyhouse, Baldoyle and Leopardstown that year, but his most important trophy was the Power Gold Cup at Punchestown. The year closed with 23 winners for the Mullins stable.

During this year Paddy was approached at his home one night by two men who had a proposition for him. Sean Flood and Tony Murphy wanted to know if Paddy would train a horse called Secret Venture for a third share. The horse had a history of heart trouble, was cheap to acquire as a result and came of a good family. 'I had not too many horses at the time so I said I would take the chance,' says Paddy. 'In fact, his heart never came against him. He was a good horse and went on to win races. I never knew what price he was bought for. I didn't have to pay anything. I know he was sold on to an owner in England for big money. He was a very good-looking horse from a good family.' At Leopardstown on 19 November 1966, Secret Venture won his first race when Sandy Barclay steered him to victory in the Cabinteely Stakes. It was to be the first of eight wins over two seasons. Says Paddy, 'To me it proved yet again that there is nothing certain in racing except uncertainty.'

One of the highlights of 1967 for the Mullins stable was when Vulpine won the Irish Grand National on Easter Monday, 1967, and this was to be followed by other significant National Hunt wins for the yard. The following year, Herring Gull also won the Irish Grand National, the second year in a row that the yard took the prize. That year, 1968, also saw Herring Gull winning the Totalisator Champion Novices' Chase, the first ever Mullins win at the Cheltenham Festival. The wins in the Irish Grand National by Vulpine and Herring Gull were to be followed over the years by two further wins for the Goresbridge stable in this prestigious event. Dim Wit was to win the race in 1972, followed close on a decade later by Luska, in 1981.

The day that Vulpine took the biggest prize in his career will be forever etched in the memories of Paddy Mullins and of the horse's connections. Vulpine was owned by Tom Nicholson, who was also the owner of Crosspatrick, which Paddy Mullins rode to victory at Naas on his return from honeymoon in 1954. It was appropriate that Nicholson, who had been with Paddy in his lean years, should also have such a fine win in the Irish Grand National in the trainer's more successful period.

The Irish Grand National had been dominated since 1960 by the trainer Tom Dreaper, who had scored an incredible seven successive wins in the race. But in 1967 Dreaper's Thorngate was missing from the starting line-up and San Jacinto started clear favourite, with Vulpine always a steady 7–1. The hero of the race had to be Vulpine's jockey, the late Matt Curran. He broke a leather during the race but still managed to keep up momentum. Rounding the bend into the straight, there was little to choose between Vulpine and Greek Vulgan, with Corrie Vacool hanging on and San Jacinto beginning to make up ground on the leaders. Corrie Vacool fell at the second last, badly hampering Curran. Despite Vulpine veering towards the rails because of the lost iron, Curran, showing great skill and courage, kept his mount going for a convincing three length win. Reynard's Heir got up to be second in front of Fort Ord, with Greek Vulgan fourth. Vulpine had some leg trouble and it finally came against him and he was off for a year or so after the race. He came back to win at Limerick at Christmas 1969 but shortly after that win he sadly developed tetanus and died, in retirement, in his owner's stable. In 1994 Matt Curran, who lived in the Goresbridge area, was to die at a tragically early age. He was only in his fifties when he passed away.

During the 1960s Andrew MacMurrough Kavanagh came to work in the Mullins yard. He was the grandson of Major MacMurrough Kavanagh, who had hunted with Paddy's father in the Mount Loftus Harriers. Andrew had been to an English public school, Milton Abbey, but had left at the age of 16, obviously deciding that the horses were preferable to the academic life. He became Paddy's amateur rider for a time, and rode a number of winners for the yard. He went on to be associated with other trainers, including Phonsie O'Brien and Paddy Sleator and turned professional in 1972. He had a good horse in training with Paddy, Captain Freaney, who won several races. His own son Morgan has also ridden out at the Mullins yard.

Says Andrew, 'Paddy was a wonderful man to work for, a most genuine, honest man. His ability to assess a horse was phenomenal. I have always thought he could tell more about a horse by just looking at him than anybody I have ever met or am likely to meet. He was able to pick up on every little nuance that a horse was able to communicate . . . '

CHAPTER 4

Glory Days with 'The Gull'

It was in October 1967 that Herring Gull, one of the best horses Paddy Mullins has ever trained, came to the yard at Doninga. The horse was owned by an Englishwoman, the late Noreen Wilson, who had settled in the Doninga area and was the closest neighbour of the Mullins family. It was pure coincidence that she happened to come to live in a house next door to a man who was one of the country's up-and-coming trainers at the time, and this coincidence was to play a role in Paddy Mullins getting Herring Gull. Mrs Wilson was the daughter of a landowner in England who had fought as an officer in the British Army all during the war but who was killed shortly after the conflict in a tractor accident on his farm. Noreen had married Captain Jock Wilson and they had lived for a time in a country residence in the Bagenalstown area, just a few miles from Doninga. Her sister Diana married the trainer Fred Winter. Then, after the break-up of her marriage to Jock, Noreen and her two sons came to live in a house near the Mullins yard.

Noreen Wilson was deeply involved in the Pony Club in Carlow and she used to bring the Mullins children to the club. Her own sons James and Robbie used to ride out in the Mullins stable and later James was to become Paddy's amateur jockey for a while. Perhaps that early experience of riding under the watchful eye of the Doninga maestro was to stand James in good stead in later years, for he was to win the Cheltenham

Gold Cup in 1980 on Little Owl, a horse he owned with his brother. During that same festival he rode Willy Wumpkins to victory for the third year running in the Coral Hurdle. And the following year James was to win the Ritz Trophy at Cheltenham for champion jockey, although he was still an amateur.

In the mid-to-late 1960s, Mrs Wilson had horses with the Irish trainer Georgie Wells, who had had considerable success with them. But, as happens sometimes between owners and trainers, there was a disagreement between herself and Mr Wells and so she asked Paddy Mullins if he would consider taking the horses. Since she was a friend of himself and Maureen and a next door neighbour, he felt he could not refuse. After establishing that he would be able to take the horses, Mrs Wilson subsequently severed her connections with Georgie Wells and phoned Paddy to tell him to collect the animals from Mr Wells's yard. And so Herring Gull came to Doninga.

Recalls Paddy, 'Inside of 24 hours of Herring Gull coming here, he won the Independent Cup at Leopardstown with the trainer listed as P. Mullins. I disclaimed any credit for training him to the press and I would not take the percentages. I insisted that Georgie should get whatever was going. Herring Gull did the business that day and he went on and did everything we asked of him.' Paddy's son Tony remembers the Independent Cup as a child – but not for anything to do with racing. 'I was only five or six at the time and I remember the Independent Cup was huge. It was really high off the ground but if you could get up and get into the cup, you could actually hide in it.' The victory in the Independent Cup event was just one of 25 winners recorded by the Mullins stable in 1967.

The following year, 1968, was certainly a year to remember for the yard, especially so far as Herring Gull was concerned. His glittering prizes were to include the Champion Novice Chase at Cheltenham, the Irish Grand National and the Jameson Gold Cup. In February that year, Herring Gull showed excellent form with an easy win in the Milltown Chase at Leopardstown. Starting at 7–2, he was always going well and moving smoothly through the field, he took charge at the final fence and won as he liked. He beat Airsprite and Edward by six lengths and three quarters of a length. His performance was so impressive that plans were made for a trip to Cheltenham. Hopes for a good performance at the festival received a slight setback when he fell at his next race on 6 March at Leopardstown. It was a four-horse race and Herring Gull appeared to have it sewn up when he came a cropper.

But later that same month, on 19 March, he was to give his connections the thrill of their lives by winning the Totalisator Champion Novices Chase, over three miles, at the Cheltenham Festival. This premier festival in the National Hunt calendar has always attracted a huge following from Ireland and that year was no exception. The Irish cheered lustily as their banker obliged. During the race, Herring Gull was always well placed by jockey John Crowley and after the second last the race had developed into a contest between four horses – Herring Gull, Playlord, Gay Trip and Freddie Boy. At the turn for home, Crowley drove Herring Gull through on the rails and running strongly up the notorious finishing hill won in very convincing fashion from Gay Trip and Freddie Boy, the winning margins being six lengths and two lengths.

Since his first entry at Cheltenham, Paddy had had to wait six years to make the breakthrough but the wait for his first win at the festival had been worth it. He was overjoyed to see Herring Gull 'do the biz'. The conditions were exactly right for the horse. Paddy recalls, 'I have never seen Cheltenham as hard as it was that year, the ground was like iron, and that suited Herring Gull. That would have been our first win at Cheltenham and it was very thrilling. After he won at Cheltenham, they all said he would win the Irish Grand National and he did so very shortly afterwards, carrying a good bit of weight. He won at Punchestown as well that year, in the John Jameson Gold Cup. He was a right good horse and there was not a pick on him. He used to train up thinner than a greyhound.'

It had been a brave decision by Paddy Mullins to go for the

Irish Grand National as Herring Gull looked to have the valuable Power Gold Cup at his mercy. But the decision to go for the longer and tougher Grand National proved to be the correct one. In the latter stages of the thrilling race, Herring Gull and Knockaney drew clear from the rest of the field. They jumped the last two together and were locked together all the way up the straight. Just as Knockaney looked to have gained the advantage, John Crowley drove Herring Gull home to win by a neck from Ben Hannon's mount. Splash came through eight lengths adrift of the first two. Herring Gull's victory in the Irish Grand National was the highlight of the stable's 31 winners that year. Paddy Mullins had left no doubt in anybody's mind but that his stable was now one to contend with for major National Hunt events, both at home and across the channel.

After the Grand National, Herring Gull went to Tralee to run in the Havasnack Plate but developed leg trouble and was out for a year. Says Paddy, 'He probably did damage, which often happens, on the hard ground in the National and in Cheltenham, and it doesn't show until the first bit of work when you bring the horse back in the following season – it happens all the time.' Herring Gull's comeback run was at Fairyhouse, on 27 December 1969, in the Christmas Handicap chase. The event would normally have been held at Leopardstown but the complex there was being re-built at the time.

The connections were to be disappointed by Herring Gull's performance in the race. He was pulled up after just one mile. But the following year, 1970, the horse was back with a bang. This was to be the year that Herring Gull would give Paddy Mullins his first ever win in France. The horse's owner, Mrs Wilson, was eager to see him run at Auteuil. The horse was sent for a couple of weeks preparation to the yard, in Chantilly, of John Ciechanowski who was no stranger to Ireland. Ciechanowski came from a once-wealthy Polish family who had lost their possessions during the Second World War. A colourful character, the story is told about him that he was once so excited about setting out to ride in the Aintree Grand

Still his favourite! Paddy with his first trophy, won in a children's pony event on his horse 'Bobby' in 1931 when aged 11.
(SEAN BOYNE)

Paddy riding Jurisprudence at the Carlow Hunt Point-to-Point in the early 1950s.

Paddy 'Sparky' Brennan leads in Flash Parade II with Paddy up after winning the Levins Moore Chase at Fairyhouse on 24 March 1953.

Paddy riding his first winner as a trainer on Flash Parade II
(No. 3, second from left) *at Punchestown to take the La Touche*
Memorial Cup on 29 April 1953.

Height O' Fashion, ridden by R. Moylan, wins the Fanfare
Handicap at the Phoenix Park on 3 May 1961.

Matt Curran on Vulpine during his Irish Grand National win at Fairyhouse on Easter Monday, 27 March 1967.

Luska, another Irish Grand National winner for Paddy on Easter Monday, 20 April 1981, ridden here by his son, George, to victory in the Ulster Bank Novice Chase at Clonmel on 9 December 1980. (LIAM HEALY)

MARCH 18TH 1969

CHELTENHAM

tote

THE TOTALISATOR CHAMPION NOVICES' STEEPLECHASE

Herring Gull - winner of the 1968 Totalisator Champion Novices' Chase

The programme cover for the 1969 Cheltenham meeting on 18 March showing Paddy's Herring Gull, winner of the Totalisator Champion Novices' Chase the previous year. He followed this win with Paddy's second Irish Grand National in a row at Fairyhouse on Easter Monday, 15 April 1968.

Matt Curran on Dim Wit, Paddy's third Irish Grand National winner; Fairyhouse, Easter Monday, 3 April 1972.

Maureen winning easily on Razzo Forte in a race for trainers' wives and daughters at Gowran Park in 1982.

Dawn Run leads Desert Orchid over a hurdle during her Champion Hurdle win at the Cheltenham Festival on 13 March 1984.

Jonjo O'Neill, Mrs Hill and Maureen after Dawn Run's victory in the Champion Hurdle. (GERRY CRANHAM)

The late Mrs Charmian Hill and her son Oliver lead in Dawn Run after the mare had won the French Champion Hurdle at Auteuil on 22 June 1984.

National that he gave an impromptu speech to his fellow jockeys about the glories of the day! He had lived in Ireland and had been an assistant trainer with Vincent O'Brien.

During the summer of 1970 Paddy and Maureen Mullins attended the wedding of jockey Tommy Carberry to Pamela Moore, daughter of the trainer Dan Moore and sister of trainer Arthur Moore and they went straight to France from the wedding reception. Entirely by chance, Paddy and Maureen found themselves staying in the same small hotel in Chantilly as jockey/trainer David Nicholson. They had not met before and were introduced by Ciechanowski. With Nicholson was his wife Dinah and the couple were on their way back from a holiday in Europe. Also staying in the hotel was David's father, the legendary jockey and trainer 'Frenchie' Nicholson.

Paddy got on extremely well with old Frenchie, who tutored many young jockeys who were to become household names and whose nickname derived from the years he had spent in France as a youth. Bobby Hall-Dare and his daughter Clody were also staying at the same hotel, which was convenient to the Millbank yard where their horse Nor was stabled during his own campaign in Paris at this period. Clody recalls how Paddy and Frenchie would reminisce about the racing game far into the night. She recalls, 'I remember a very good evening listening to the two of them in the hotel restaurant. There were some great stories told that night. They were topping each other's stories. The humour was marvellous.' Frenchie Nicholson would have had plenty to talk about – it was said of him that as a rider he won every race that was open to him on the Cheltenham Festival card and then won a few more as a trainer.

The French jockey that Paddy had lined up to school Herring Gull was injured in a fall but right there in his hotel in Chantilly, Paddy had a replacement. Following his chance encounter with the man from Doninga, David 'The Duke' Nicholson, later to be one of the most prominent trainers in England, schooled Herring Gull over the French fences and then went on to ride him in the Prix de Saint Sanseur at Auteuil. This race was regarded as a 'preparation' for the real target of the expedition, the notoriously gruelling Grand Steeplechase de Paris, known to the French as 'le Grand Steep'. Herring Gull ran well at first in the 'prep' event, but had to be pulled up. Nicholson was to maintain his links with the horse, travelling to Ireland the following year to ride Herring Gull in the Galway Plate and finishing fifth.

David Nicholson has vivid memories of that early connection with Paddy Mullins. 'I remember the time well,' 'The Duke' recalls. 'I was still riding at the time and was delighted even to school the horse to keep my hand in. So I was really glad when the chance came to ride Herring Gull in the Prix de Saint Sanseur and was very disappointed with the result, as I had to pull him up but in the long run he was to pay for his trip. I went over to Ireland the following year to ride the horse in the Galway Plate for Paddy and finished fifth, so far as I can recall. That was about 25 years ago, and over the years I have come to know Paddy Mullins well. I have a very high opinion of him, not just as a horse trainer but as a man. Paddy's horses will always be fit and well-schooled. His record over the years, particularly with Dawn Run, is something of which he can be justly proud. It may be equalled in time but up to now Paddy's record at Cheltenham is unique.' It's not a bad compliment coming from Nicholson, who is no mean operator himself when it comes to turning out the winners at Cheltenham. 'The Duke', in his familiar sheepskin coat and trilby hat, was very much in evidence in the winner's enclosure during the 1995 meeting. He trained three of the winners, including Viking Flagship who took the Queen Mother Champion Chase title for the second year in a row.

Some days after the 'prep' outing in Auteuil, in which David Nicholson partnered Herring Gull, there came the really stiff challenge for the Irish horse that Sunday – the 'Grand Steep' itself, on 21 June. For the big race, Paddy had called on the services of the veteran English jockey, Stan Mellor who, over the years, had been noted for his rivalry with Fred Winter for the title of National Hunt champion jockey. The two of them monopolised the championship for eight of the ten years from

1953 to 1962. Stan took the title on three occasions and during his riding career he was to enter the winner's circle no fewer than 1,034 times.

Stan was also noted for his quality of 'indestructibility' and it was just as well, for he was to have a really bad fall in the 'Grand Steep'. Herring Gull never really got into the race and fell at the big ditch, with both horse and rider lucky to emerge without serious injury. The horse's connections were very disappointed, as was Paddy Mullins himself. Stan was also scheduled to ride Herring Gull in the Prix des Drags at the same Auteuil track the following Wednesday, the 'consolation race' for the 'Grand Steep'. But Paddy reckoned that Stan had taken such a bad fall that he would decline to come back for the ride. However, the veteran English rider was made of sterner stuff.

Stan Mellor recalls that time in France vividly. 'I had ridden Herring Gull for Paddy previously at Punchestown, and he was a big, weak horse. He was, as Paddy himself said, of the greyhound breed. He was very aptly named – he was really thin. I remember falling at the big ditch in the "Grand Steep" on the Sunday, and I do know that Paddy did not believe I would want to come back for Wednesday's race. But the thought of pulling out never crossed my mind.' Paddy had to go back to Ireland because there were other horses there needing his attention, but he left Herring Gull in Paris, in Ciechanowski's yard, in the capable hands of a lad from the Doninga stable, Michael Brennan. And Stan Mellor did come back to ride the horse in the Prix des Drags – with marvellous results. This time, the partnership won.

Says Stan, 'I remember coming up to the fifth, the big ditch that brought us down the previous Sunday. But this time we got across safely, and soon we were home and dry. It was marvellous to win that race. Herring Gull was a good one and he gave me the biggest win of my career. The prize money that day was £7,518 and if you equate that with the prize money for that year's Hennessy Gold Cup which was £5,700, you will understand how big the race was and how delighted I was to win it. I had a great time in France celebrating with the owner,

Mrs Wilson and her party afterwards. I would have loved to have ridden more horses for Paddy, especially horses such as Dawn Run. Paddy was undoubtedly one of the best and his horses were always turned out in magnificent condition and were a joy to ride.'

Victory was particularly sweet for the connections that day because few of the experts had fancied Herring Gull's chances and the horse was quoted at 50–1. The satisfaction for Stan Mellor of winning such an important race was all the greater as he was coming to the end of his riding career. He retired as a jockey at the end of the 1972 season and went on to become a very successful trainer. When Paddy Mullins, back in Doninga, heard of the Auteuil victory he was ecstatic. On his first visit to Auteuil, during his honeymoon back in 1954, he had permitted himself to dream of one day fielding a runner there. Now he had actually had a winner at the prestigious track – sure evidence that sometimes dreams DO come true – especially if you persevere long enough.

Says Paddy, 'It was a terrific achievement for Stan to win the Prix des Drags. It was an important race. After his fall, I did not think he would come back to ride the horse but he did. There was tremendous jubilation and Stan was absolutely over the moon. He always says I gave him the best winner he ever had.' During Cheltenham week in 1993, the *Sporting Life* featured Paddy in its 'Lifestyles' column. Asked whom he would nominate as his racing hero, he named Stan Mellor, explaining that he did not expect Stan to ride in the Prix des Drags following 'a real creaser of a fall' three days earlier. Paddy went on, 'Stan could easily have decided that he would be better off staying at home. But not a bit of it. He flew back and won the race. That was true dedication.'

Herring Gull came home from France and was second in the Galway Plate of that year to Lisnaree. Then the horse was off again on his travels – this time across the Atlantic. The organisers of the Colonial Cup which was inaugurated that year, 1970, at Camden, South Carolina, invited Paddy Mullins to bring Herring Gull to take part in the race, all expenses paid.

Few Irish trainers took horses to America in those days and it was Paddy's first trip there. Unfortunately, the trip was to end in terrible disappointment. Paddy had a 'no run' with Herring Gull due to the horse's erratic behaviour on the day. There are two posts at the start and Herring Gull, with John Crowley up, ducked to the outside of one of the posts at the 'off'. The starter brought all the horses back but Herring Gull ducked out for a second time and was out of the race. Even though the trip did not cost anything to owner or trainer, the 'no run' was still a huge disappointment. Paddy Mullins could only wonder what might have been had the horse actually run that day. He says, 'I thought the race was made for Herring Gull. The ground and the fences were exactly right for him.'

While the visit did not bring the success Paddy had hoped for, it was a memorable trip from other points of view. The Irish visitors were entertained royally, their American hosts sparing nothing in their hospitality. 'We were under a huge marquee one night for one of the receptions,' recalls Paddy, 'and we were told that the roof of the marquee was made from the parachute that the men who had made the moon landing had used on their return to earth. I was never able to check if this was true, but at least it was a good story.'

Some months later, Herring Gull was unplaced to Persian War in the Sweeps Hurdle at Leopardstown. He was ultimately to leave the Mullins yard for England. James Wilson, son of the owner, was starting out on his career as a rider and went to David Nicholson to learn the 'trade' and the horse went with him. Herring Gull ran in races in England but was never the same force again. 'I have an idea that the horse got fed up,' says Paddy Mullins. 'It happens to many of them. They either break down or they get fed up.'

Noreen Wilson has passed away but Paddy and Maureen Mullins still keep in touch with James Wilson, now a trainer near Cheltenham, although they usually only meet during festival week. When Paddy and Maureen go to Cheltenham every year they always stay in the same farmhouse, owned by friends and neighbours of James. They stayed there even before it became a guest house, as it is now. On each of the three days of the festival, James Wilson gives a big lunch party at his home in Ham Hill and leading figures in the racing world attend every year. Over the years, around the table one would have found leading jockeys like Peter Scudamore, or leading trainers like Fred Winter. Paddy and Maureen Mullins attend one of the lunch parties every year and the occasion gives them a chance to meet old friends. They usually meet David Nicholson, with whom they have been friendly since he rode Herring Gull in 1970. To everyone in England, the host of these parties is known as Jim, but to the Mullins family he will always be known as James – the name by which he was known when he lived at Doninga. No doubt the annual get-together revives memories of great days in decades past, and the glory years of Herring Gull.

* * *

As Paddy Mullins forged ahead with his National Hunt horses, he was also extremely busy with the Flat horses in his yard. He still has vivid memories of Robert Hall-Dare's horse Nor, one of the best Flat horses in his stable in the late 1960s and early 1970s. Oddly enough, despite his very good record on the Flat, the horse didn't have the kind of impressive pedigree that one might expect. He was, in fact, of National Hunt breeding. Nor won his first race on 2 August 1969 at Baldoyle when, with Johnny Roe up, he won the Claremont Stakes. (This was to be one of a total of 23 winners recorded by the Mullins stable that year.) Nor ended the season on a very high note when he took the valuable Birdcatcher Nursery handicap at Naas on 11 October. His early form as a three-year-old saw him twice fourth and then, on 4 May 1970, he showed vastly improved form when, in a great finish to the Hardicanute Stakes at Navan, he was beaten a head and a short head by French Score and Mackintosh.

In line with Robert Hall-Dare's adventurous policy of sending his horses to race abroad, Paddy Mullins then took Nor off to Paris, where he was stabled in Charlie Millbank's yard in Chantilly. Nor was in France about the same time as Herring Gull. Nor, partnered by colourful English-born jockey Buster Parnell, won an 11 furlong race at Maisons-Laffitte, beating The Swell by two lengths. Mr Hall-Dare's daughter Clody recalls that Nor won the race on the very day that he arrived in France. If the horse was tired from the journey, he didn't let it affect his performance. Clearly, Nor must have been extremely fit. During a three week sojourn in Paris, Nor was placed third in another race, the Prix du Lys at Chantilly over the same distance. Nor was then brought back to the Mullins stable, to get just over two weeks preparation for the Irish Derby on Saturday, 27 June 1970. In this great international Classic race at The Curragh, Nor would be taking on what was already being hailed as 'the horse of the century', Nijinsky. The Vincent O'Brien-trained Nijinsky was to start at odds-on favourite, while Nor was to start at 66–1.

Paddy was hoping to get Buster Parnell to ride Nor in this major race, as he knew the horse well. However, Buster opted instead to take Charlie Weld's horse Ringsend, a 33–1 chance. Even though Buster was fully entitled to choose another mount, Paddy could not but feel disappointed. At the same time, he could never really get annoyed with Buster. Says Paddy, 'Buster was a lovely fellow. He was a real Cockney with all the East End lingo and we got on very well together.' Paddy called in a young Australian jockey, Alan Simpson, to ride Nor in the race, worth almost £53,000.

Nijinsky, ridden by Liam Ward, won the race, but Nor came a very creditable fourth, finishing within six lengths of the superstar winner. Paddy had Nor in the form of his life that day and to run the great Nijinsky so close was a considerable achievement for the stable. There was some surprise at Nor's very good performance but Paddy and Mr Hall-Dare had expected him to run well. Nor also picked up some good money on the day, as there was a sizable prize for fourth place. Buster had made the wrong choice – his mount finished way behind, coming ninth in the field of 13. Meadowville, ridden by Lester Piggott, was second and Master Guy third.

Mr Hall-Dare was still ready to travel with Nor, and the horse went to Sandown Park in July to run in the Eclipse Stakes, taking on some of the best Flat horses in training. He finished third to Connaught and Karabas, and went on to give a very impressive performance when running Riboprince to half a length in the Blandford Stakes at The Curragh. Nor continued to campaign outside Ireland as a four-year-old, his best performance being in the Coronation Cup at Ascot when he finished fourth. Later in the season, in September, he crossed to Scotland and turned in a magnificent weight-carrying performance. Shouldering 9st 10lb, he took fifth place behind Goodison in the Ayrshire Handicap.

At home Nor had two successes, the first at Leopardstown in the Killiney Handicap on 12 June and three weeks later at the Phoenix Park, when he won the CBA Cup. In the latter event he carried 9st 13lb, leading commentators to describe him as the best ten furlong handicapper in the country. During that period, Nor made an unsuccessful trip to Germany, being taken there by Paddy's nephew Brian, who was to ride a number of winners for the stable in the 1970s.

Nor's stablemate and half brother, Lucky Drake, also owned by Mr Hall-Dare, made his debut in 1970 but his career was not quite as distinguished as Nor's. He registered his first win on 10 April 1971 in the Grafton Stakes at the Phoenix Park, ridden by Johnny Roe. He followed this with a win at Leopardstown on 8 May in the Boston Handicap. His best ever performance came later that year in the Irish Sweeps Derby at The Curragh. Ridden by Thomas Murphy, he finished fourth to Irish Ball, the second year in a row Paddy had supplied the Derby fourth. The prize money was £4,000 – a considerable sum in those days. Once again, the experts had underestimated the ability of the Mullins entry in the big race, Lucky Drake being quoted at 100–1.

The owner's daughter Clody Norton says that while Nor was in with a chance to win the Derby, his stablemate Lucky Drake was never seen as having a serious chance of a win – but it was reckoned that he could do well enough to qualify for place money and, of course, this was the outcome on the day. Lucky Drake then ran another good race in the Irish St Leger, finishing third. Later that month he was off to Scotland where he won impressively at Ayr. Both Nor and Lucky Drake left Paddy's stable at the end of their four-year-old careers and were sold to America by Mr Hall-Dare. Nor was purchased by Jimmy Canty, who was based in California, and who was the brother of a renowned Irish jockey Joe Canty. Nor went on to win some races as well as having moderate success as a stallion.

Paddy recalls with amusement the time that Nor was entered for a race in Deauville, in northern France, and how panic almost ensued when it was thought that jockey Buster Parnell had got lost en route. Paddy tells how he and Maureen, accompanied by Mr Hall-Dare and Buster, set off for London en route to France. 'We spent the night in a hotel at London Heathrow. When it came to breakfast – no sign of Buster. A fellow answered the phone in what we thought was his room and roundly abused us for waking him up. Came the time to go to the plane and we had to go and leave without Buster. We flew to Paris and hired a car to take us to Deauville and went straight to the stable yard to see the horse. I was worried for I thought I was going to have to find another jockey. But when we arrived at the stable, who was there waiting for us but Buster.

'He told us how his room had been changed, and that the people at reception were trying to phone him in the wrong room. He had woken up late, realised he had missed the plane, wondered how he was going to get to Deauville, looked up the newspaper, saw that Geoff Lewis was riding at the same meeting, rung his wife at home in Ireland, got Geoff Lewis's number, rung Geoff at home, told him his plight and Geoff had come to the rescue. It turns out that Geoff's boss had a small plane hired for the day to go to Deauville, so Buster hitched a ride on the plane, and landed in Deauville while we were only landing in Paris. We could not believe it when we walked into the stable yard in Deauville and there was Buster. We didn't win the race in Deauville, unfortunately. Buster presently lives in Denmark. His son David served his time with me and rode some winners. He was a grand chap and a lovely rider. Tragically, he was killed in a car accident a couple of years ago.'

CHAPTER 5

Nothing Dimwitted about this Horse

Veterinary surgeon Jerry O'Neill was celebrating his wedding when a relative bet him a fiver he'd never ride a winner. The stake money was given for safe keeping to Maureen Mullins, who was a guest at the reception along with her husband Paddy. The fiver bet was a standing joke among family and friends for years. Amateur jockey Jerry O'Neill was ultimately to collect on the bet in January, 1970 when he rode his own horse Dim Wit to victory in the Maynooth Stakes at Naas. Jerry was ecstatic. It was his first win and Dim Wit's first win. But the horse, trained by Paddy Mullins, was to go on and do an even bigger favour for his connections. Just a couple of years later, Dim Wit was to win the Irish Grand National. Despite the name, there was nothing dimwitted about this animal when it came to winning the big one. Dim Wit proved to be one of the best horses in training at the Mullins stable in the early 1970s.

Jerry O'Neill came from Athy, Co. Kildare. His father was in the Indian Civil Service, and he spent a lot of time in his younger days with his uncle, Joe Mallick, a prominent trainer at the time on The Curragh, and it was there that he developed his love of horses. He came to practise as a vet in Borris, Co. Carlow, and became friendly with Paddy Mullins. He decided he would like to have a horse in training. Paddy told him about a foal by Star Signal that the late Mrs Alice Brown had for sale in Bagenalstown. Says Paddy, 'Jerry and I went and saw the foal. It was Dim Wit. Jerry, who had land near Borris where he trains now, bought him and reared him and produced him and made him what he was. After being trained by Jerry for a while he came here when he started to run as a four-year-old.'

Dim Wit, who had been bought for a very modest price, turned out to be a very good horse. After the horse's first win at Naas, he went on to win three hurdle races and the following year, 1971, took to 'chasing in great style. He won a novice 'chase at Fairyhouse in February, and went on to win another 'chase at Naas the following month. On 20 April, ridden by H. R. Beasley, he won the John Jameson Cup at Punchestown. In early 1972 he won two 'chases, including the Thyestes Cup at Gowran Park. His progress as a 'chaser was so impressive that it was decided to let him have a go at the Cheltenham Gold Cup. David Mould was Dim Wit's rider in the prestigious event. But the outing was to end in keen disappointment for Paddy and the connections. Dim Wit never finished the race. He was pulled up, the jockey saying he felt there was something wrong with the horse. Says Paddy Mullins, 'We were very disappointed at the time, and we could not understand what was wrong.' The race was won that year by Glencaraig Lady.

When Dim Wit turned out for the Irish Grand National before a huge Bank Holiday crowd the following Easter Monday, there was not a great deal of public confidence in him because of being pulled up at Cheltenham. The well-backed favourite was The Dikler, who was third in the Gold Cup. But Dim Wit was to confound the doubters on the day by turning in a peerless performance. On this occasion, it was The Dikler's turn to be pulled up. Dim Wit wasn't among the horses that made the early running. Beggar's Way was in front jumping the third last with Veuve moving into second place and Dim Wit moving into third. Veuve fell at the second last and on the run to the final fence, Dim Wit forged up on the far side to clear the fence in front of Beggar's Way. Matt Curran pressed on with Dim Wit to score an easy victory, and to give the Mullins yard its third Irish Grand National victory in just six years. The *Irish Field* commented that great credit was due to the trainer Paddy

Mullins, and remarked that Dim Wit had compensated fully for being pulled up at Cheltenham.

The following year Dim Wit dropped dead after a race at Punchestown. It emerged that the horse had a heart problem. Paddy realised now why David Mould had pulled him up at Cheltenham. 'Obviously Mould was right when he sensed there was something wrong with the horse. Mould would never abuse a horse. But for his pulling up Dim Wit in the Gold Cup, we might not have won the Grand National a few weeks later.'

The early 1970s proved to be a particularly good period for the Mullins stable. The year 1971 provided the yard with the biggest haul of winners to date, a total of 51, an average of one a week. It was a far cry from the days of an average of one winner a year! The following year, 1972, the tally had increased by one. Lock Diamond was a successful horse for the Mullins stable at this period. It was also during this period in the early 1970s that one of the best horses of the decade came to the Mullins yard – Brendon's Road. The horse belonged to an American woman, Dotsie Rudkin, who, along with her husband Henry Rudkin Jnr used to spend part of the year in their country residence in Co. Carlow. The rest of the year they spent in America.

It was in 1953 that Dotsie's wealthy parents-in-law, Margaret and Henry Rudkin Snr visited Ireland for the first time. They planned to do some salmon fishing – and they also wanted to find any surviving traces of Henry's Anglo-Irish ancestry. Henry Snr was a stockbroker and Margaret was a very well-known figure in America. She had started baking wholemeal bread at home in the 1930s and had built up the business into a multi-million dollar concern called the Pepperidge Farm Company. They had been told that a Rudkin ancestor was buried in the Cathedral of St Laserian in the Leighlinbridge area of Co. Carlow and they wanted to find the grave.

On a warm sunny day they drove out of Dublin and found the cathedral, part of which dates from the twelfth century. In the floor of the nave they found the tomb of the first Henry

Rudkin, who went from England to Ireland in the seventeenth century, founded the Anglo-Irish branch of the family, and died in 1726 at the age of 101. One of the Rudkins had built a fine house in this area of Co. Carlow in 1704 and it had been in the family for 150 years, until the family emigrated to America in 1855. Henry and Margaret Rudkin located this old manor house, found it just happened to be up for sale and bought it on the spur of the moment, thus re-establishing the Rudkin connection with the area and with the house, after a lapse of 100 years. The couple would spend part of the year at their home in Connecticut and the rest of the year at their very fine country residence in Co. Carlow, Corries House. Sometimes the Rudkins would travel from America by ship, docking at Cobh, or sometimes they would fly into Shannon.

In the late 1960s and into the 1970s, the couple's son Henry Jnr and his wife Dotsie were also spending a lot of time at Corries House, their Irish ancestral home. They were interested in horses and Dotsie's two brothers, the Bostwicks, had been prominent amateur jockeys and racehorse owners in England. Dotsie Rudkin was to become the owner of one of the most successful horses trained by Paddy Mullins during the 1970s, Brendon's Road. Despite the horse's fine record of wins, Paddy is convinced that Brendon's Road never realised its full potential because of an injury. He can only speculate on what might have been had Brendon's Road, who came second in the Sweeps Hurdle one year, remained uninjured.

Paddy recalls, 'Dotsie Rudkin was a very good client. She and her husband Henry would usually spend the summer at Corries House. They spent a lot of money doing it up. The house is about three miles from Doninga as the crow flies, across the Barrow, over in Tom Foley, Danoli country. They were grand people. They fitted in very well into the hunting and racing scene here. They were friends of the Vigors family, who ran Burgage Stud. They said to myself or Maureen that they would like to have a racehorse. So I went to the Ballsbridge Sales and picked out this one for them – he was Brendon's Road.

'He wasn't the apple of everybody's eye on the day of the sales. The reason I went for him was that his sire was Roadhouse and I thought this was a very good sire. Roadhouse wasn't a popular stallion but he had produced a very good horse Moonduster, which was owned by a friend of ours, Michael Ronayne, so I said to myself that Brendon's Road would be fine for me. He was slightly back of his knees – which can sometimes lead to tendon trouble. This put off a lot of would-be buyers and thus brought down the price and made him easier to buy. I felt that in this particular case the slight 'back of the knees' characteristic should not be a serious problem and this turned out to be the case. Brendon's Road, who was out of Brendonian, turned out to be a smashing horse. It was the Rudkins' first racehorse and they had a lot of enjoyment out of it.'

Brendon's Road had his first win on 4 March 1971, when Brian Mullins rode him to victory in the Corinthian Plate at Thurles. From that first victory, he went on to win a total of 14 races on the flat, over hurdles and over fences. His last win was in March 1976 when he won the Meath Chase at Navan. Paddy Mullins is convinced he would have been an even better horse but for an accident while running in the Players Amateur race in Galway in 1973. Recalls Paddy, 'Unfortunately coming round the final bend he was struck into by another horse, cut a fetlock and it took months to get him right. Even though he raced again, and won again, I thought he was never the same horse after that. Meeting with an accident like that is one of these things that happen in racing. Ted Walsh, who has since made his name as a leading racing commentator on TV, was riding him that day, the only time Ted ever rode for me and I thought Ted gave him a really great ride. Brendon's Road was fourth in that race.'

Dotsie Rudkin also had a filly called Topless Dancer in training with Paddy in the 1970s, who won races on the Flat. As regards Brendon's Road, after his career on the racecourse came to a close, he was ridden by Paddy's son Willy in point-to-point events. Meanwhile the Rudkins sold Corries House and resumed permanent residence in the USA. Says Paddy, 'They are still living in America but we have not run into them for quite a while and they seem to have dropped out of racing.' On the wall of the Mullins's drawing room at Doninga, there is a memento of the Rudkins and of Brendon's Road. A mirror with a silver frame in the shape of a horse shoe, bearing the name of Brendon's Road, is inscribed to Paddy and Maureen Mullins, from Dotsie and Henry Rudkin.

Corries House continued its own links with racing after it was bought in the late 1970s by the colourful trainer Denny Cordell-Lavarack, who was also a major figure in the international rock music business. Cordell-Lavarack, whom Paddy knew slightly, died in February 1995 at the young age of 51. He was a friend of the Rolling Stones and had helped to shape the fortunes of such artists as Georgie Fame, T Rex, Bob Marley and, more recently, the Cranberries. Says Paddy, 'Cordell-Lavarack had a terrific good patch as a trainer and then as often happens, he went through a lean period. But he had the music to make his money from. When he first came to live in Corries it was greyhounds he was involved in. I knew him to say hello to. He was a nice man.'

Apart from Brendon's Road, there are a number of horses from this period that stand out in the memory of Paddy Mullins. One of these is Kiltotan. The horse was bred and owned by the late John Gavin. Kiltotan had a series of hurdle wins that resulted in the owner getting some attractive offers for the horse. But all the offers were turned down. Says Paddy, 'John was near retirement at the time and loved to see his horse running and would be absolutely thrilled with a win. He refused all offers for Kiltotan saying, "I am as much entitled to have a good horse as anyone else." Eventually the horse was killed. Some would say it's best to be sorry for selling than not selling. But John was always happy to keep Kiltotan and pass up on the good money that was being offered for the horse.'

Desu Barker is another fine performer from this period. During 1974 he clocked up three hurdle wins, in addition to his two wins from the previous year. Says Paddy, 'Desu Barker was a very good horse, but like all good horses the handicapper caught up with him and he got too much weight.' Desu Barker, owned by Tom Ruane, had one expedition abroad during 1974 – to the French racecourse of Evry, an unusual venue for an Irish horse. Ridden by Willy Mullins, he came fourth in the race, which was for amateurs. After all the excitement of the previous year, 1974 proved to be a comparatively quiet one for Paddy Mullins. During the year he saddled 39 winners. Most of his wins were over jumps, but he had, in the meantime, scored a truly notable victory on the Flat . . .

CHAPTER 6

A Tribute from Lester

Dr Malcolm Thorpe will always remember how his Paddy Mullins-trained mare Hurry Harriet won one of the most prestigious Flat races in England, the £50,000 Champion Stakes in Newmarket. A native of Kilgreaney, Co. Carlow, just about a mile as the crow flies across the River Barrow from the Mullins stables at Doninga, he had been working for many years as a doctor in Canada and was unable to come over for the big race in 1973. But shortly before the off, he phoned the stable at Doninga where Ann O'Neill, the housekeeper at the time, relayed the race commentary from the TV over the phone. Says Dr Thorpe, 'The young woman gave quite a good commentary to myself and my wife Anne. And then, over the phone, we could hear the young woman and one of Paddy's kids screaming with excitement. We had won the race. It was really a marvellous moment.' In fact it was Paddy's son Tom who was letting off steam. He was the only one of the Mullins children home that day.

Meanwhile in Newmarket, just after Paddy's daughter Sandra led in the winner and amid the jubilation in the parade ring, the Doninga trainer was approached briefly by one of the legends of racing. Lester Piggott, who had also ridden in the race, passed by Paddy in the ring, carrying his saddle. For a moment, the eyes of two of the quietest men in racing met. 'Well done!' grunted Lester to the Irish trainer. From the taciturn Piggott, this was fulsome praise indeed. Paddy's reply was equally brief and to the point. 'Thanks,' he said. Piggott had ridden in a couple of races at The Curragh for Paddy previously. Says Paddy, 'Piggott would be over for the Derby and would be available to ride in the other races and he rode a couple of two-year-olds for me but never rode a winner for me. We knew each other slightly, but he would never normally say a word to me.' In the Champion Stakes that day, Piggott had been riding a horse owned by the French millionaire Daniel Wildenstein. Winning the Champion Stakes was one of the high points in the career of Paddy Mullins. Hurry Harriet beat into second place that day Allez France, the top filly in Europe at the time. The win helped to underline Paddy's ability as a trainer of Flat horses. He considers Hurry Harriet to have been the best Flat horse he ever trained.

Sandra clearly recalls the day her father took on some of the biggest stables in Flat racing – and beat them. 'It was the best day of all,' she says. 'There was just myself, Ma and Da and the mare, and Ferdie Murphy who was looking after the mare. Newmarket was jammed that day with the crowds. We could not even get into the stands and we had to watch the race at the winning post. We had got separated from Ma and I could not even see the race. But I knew Hurry Harriet was coming with a run and then we realised she had won. Myself and Da ran down to the winners' enclosure and I turned around at one stage and he was up in the air with his binoculars flying roaring "haroo". I can still picture him. He never did it before – or since. We ran down and still could not find mother so my father asked me to lead Hurry Harriet in. We were brought in for champagne, just the three of us, and there were about 50 glasses laid out. They must have been expecting somebody else to win, somebody with a big entourage. We had a glass of champagne and skedaddled.'

The owner of Hurry Harriet, Dr Thorpe, had known of Paddy Mullins's prowess with horses even before the Doninga man took out a trainer's licence. Coming from the Carlow-Kilkenny border region, he was familiar with Paddy's reputation as a man who knew all there was to know about horses. 'Paddy was regarded as the best young horseman in the region,' says Dr Thorpe. 'My sisters used to hunt with him in the Mount Loftus Harriers and I knew all about his ability with horses.' Meanwhile Dr Thorpe emigrated to Canada to work as a doctor after taking out a medical degree in Trinity College, Dublin. When, in 1958, he decided he would like to have a racehorse back in Ireland, he reckoned the obvious man to help him was Paddy Mullins. Dr Thorpe arranged for his sister Sheila to phone the Doninga trainer to ask him to buy a yearling for him at Goff's sales. Dr Thorpe had already marked out two or three to be considered. Paddy bought one of these, a small filly, and so began a complicated process which was to lead ultimately to the breeding of Hurry Harriet.

Recalls Paddy, 'The small filly I bought initially, Lavandou Mink, wasn't great herself but she bred a winner. One of her other progeny was a brood mare later on and she was burned in a fire at a stud where she was visiting a stallion. Dr Thorpe asked me to replace her with the insurance money.' While on the lookout for a replacement, Paddy Mullins spotted a mare for sale in an advertisement in the *Irish Field* and he reckoned this could be just what was required. Ironically, about the same time, Dr Thorpe, who also subscribed to the *Irish Field*, spotted the same ad. When Paddy phoned to say he had come across a likely prospect, Dr Thorpe knew exactly what he was talking about – he had come to the same conclusion, that the mare in question was just what they wanted. Both men had, for many years, been keen students of pedigree and bloodlines.

Paddy travelled up to Co. Laois to see the mare, Somnambula, at Hollymount Stud, run by Mrs Mary Annesley whose son Richard was to become a well-known trainer. Somnambula had not shown any great merit in her own two races as a two-year-old. It was really because of Somnambula's sire, Chanteur I, that the decision to buy the mare was made. Says Paddy, 'Here was a mare by the sire that Malcolm would have liked the best, and on our doorstep.' In accordance with the custom that often prevails in Ireland, Paddy did not himself make the approach to Mrs Annesley to do the deal. He used an intermediary for this purpose.

The go-between in this case was the late Des Connolly, a farmer who had Lock Diamond in training at the Mullins yard. Says Paddy, 'I didn't speak to Mrs Annesley at all. I went and saw the animal, came back and mulled over it and then got in touch with Des Connolly. I said to Des, "Go and try to buy her." We do this all the time. It helps if you are not in the forefront position when you are doing the deal. If the man you are using fails, I can go in. It gives you a fall-back position. I bought a horse the other day – the same procedure was involved.'

Somnambula went in foal to a stallion which Dr Thorpe and another Irish medical man, Cork-born Dr Mike Bennett, had sent over to stand at Baroda Stud in Co. Kildare for a couple of seasons. The stallion was the oddly-named Yrrah Jr, who had only won two small races but whose pedigree was more noteworthy – he was by Ribot out of the Italian Oaks winner Ola. The foal that resulted from the union of Somnambula and Yrrah Jr (Harry spelt backwards) was Hurry Harriet, who was reared at Doninga.

Says Paddy, 'Some horses will show promise straight away, and other horses, you think they are useless, and they will keep improving and keep improving and will even turn out better than the one that was showing promise from the beginning. You can't generalise. The most extraordinary case of a horse showing early promise I came across was Hurry Harriet. She showed it from the beginning in a dramatic way. I could not believe it. She was only just barely into the riding out stage and we used to work in a big field and the horses finally would come nicely up along the field . . . and before she was any length at all at it she was streaking away. That was one case where the early promise was later fulfilled.'

Paddy's daughter Sandra remembers riding out Hurry Harriet as a filly. But after a while Sandra had to give up riding her because she was so strong. 'Hurry Harriet was extremely competitive,' says Sandra. 'When you were riding her out, she would never pull up until she had got in front of all the other horses. She was extremely fast. She was lethal.'

Hurry Harriet ran as a two-year-old in a seven and a half furlong race at Gowran Park in 1972 and, although she did not win, her jockey on the day, Johnny Roe, reckoned she had huge potential. Johnny, who was nine times Irish champion jockey on the Flat between 1963 and 1974, remarked to Paddy afterwards, 'You've a good one there.' She went on to be entered for a similar race at Gowran Park a couple of weeks later. Dr Thorpe wasn't there, but some friends of the connections decided to have a good gamble and considerable sums were wagered with the bookies, some bets going on at odds of 33–1. Hurry Harriet, ridden once again by Johnny Roe, won the race easily. A lot of money was lifted from the satchels of the disgruntled bookies and the mare's trainer began to formulate some ambitious plans for her career.

Recalls Paddy Mullins, 'Hurry Harriet went to The Curragh for what used to be called the Irish Stakes – the only race where two-year-olds took on the older horses and she confounded the handicapper by doing what she did – she won from the older horses in very heavy ground. Captain Mick Byrne was the handicapper and he thought it was the greatest performance of a two-year-old he had seen and as a result put her up near the top in the free handicap. He was slated for it and people laughed at him but he's a very good handicapper and was proven right afterwards when Hurry Harriet raced as a three-year-old.' During 1972 Dr Thorpe also had success with another horse Party Mink. He bred and reared Party Mink himself and, trained by Paddy Mullins, the horse won four races.

Hurry Harriet went on to win the Pretty Polly Stakes at The Curragh, beating the Irish One Thousand Guineas runner-up Annerbelle in the process. One of the disappointed connections of the latter horse, who obviously considered Annerbelle to be a far better bred animal than Hurry Harriet, was heard by Paddy to remark afterwards, 'Well, we can throw away the stud book now.' In the Irish Guinness Oaks, Hurry Harriet came third in a field of 12, beaten seven lengths by Dahlia and Mysterious. Then it was decided the mare would go and compete in France. In a high-class field, and ridden by Jean Cruguet, she beat all but the formidable Allez France in the Prix Vermeille at Longchamp. It was some achievement for a trainer who was still comparatively unknown on the international Flat scene.

Dr Thorpe then set his sights on the really big time and in consultation with Paddy Mullins decided to enter Hurry Harriet for the Prix de l'Arc de Triomphe at the same Paris track. Cruguet, who rode the filly in the Prix Vermeille, was, unfortunately, not available to ride Hurry Harriet in the Prix de l'Arc, having given a previous commitment to ride another, less promising horse in the race. So Dr Thorpe went to the expense of bringing over from America a young jockey who was making his name at the time, Angel Cordero. Paddy Mullins smiles as he recalls the brash young American. 'Angel Cordero was something else. He used to wear a sweat shirt with the slogan, "You don't have to go to heaven to see an angel!"' Some of the Irish contingent who came over for the race were intrigued by Cordero and his Afro hair style. They had never seen an Hispanic jockey before.

Says Paddy, 'The race turned out a disaster for us. Hurry Harriet was drawn on the outside and on the outside the ground was dreadful. And although she appeared at one stage in the race she finished out of the money.' There was a bad omen of things to come when, on the way up to the start, Hurry Harriet, who started at 96–1, ran away with her jockey. During the incident, Cordero's saddle slipped, and the filly had to be re-saddled. Recalls Dr Thorpe, 'There were 28 horses in the race and Hurry Harriet was drawn 27th on the outside. The track was cut up. Actually it was due to the Prix Vermeille which was held there about a month before. They water the courses in France and they had the course watered for the Prix Vermeille. Then they had a thunderburst the night before the Prix de l'Arc and the horses' hooves went in almost up to the hocks.

'Paddy and I walked the course and he picked out these big

sods with yellow on top where the grass had died. Paddy was not impressed by the course. He said it was not even bad going, it was false going. In the Prix de l'Arc they move the rail seven metres inwards so that maybe the first half a dozen horses will get perfect going along the rail. But Hurry Harriet was drawn on the outside. In France they are very strict about the rules, and they have lines from the start and you have to stick to the lines for about 400 metres, or they will disqualify you. The only way to get to the rail is to drop back and run along the rail. Cordero did not know the track. In retrospect, I should have let Johnny Roe ride Hurry Harriet that day.' Hurry Harriet finished 19th, whereas Allez France, to whom she was second in the Prix Vermeille, came second.

It had been a very unlucky outing for Hurry Harriet, but her owner was not a man to give up easily. Dr Thorpe said to Paddy Mullins, 'We'll go for the Champion Stakes at Newmarket.' In this Group 1 race for three-year-olds and upwards, scheduled for Saturday, 20 October 1973, Hurry Harriet would once again be coming up against her old adversary, Allez France, the most formidable filly around at that time. On the day itself few seemed to fancy Hurry Harriet's chances, having lost 10 of her previous 11 races that season, and having been twice beaten by Allez France. Hurry Harriet started at 33–1 and those odds seemed to be justified when Allez France took a clear lead and looked almost certain to win. But Hurry Harriet, ridden once again by Cruguet, leaving the rest of the field trailing, made good progress on the rails, challenged on the hill and went in front in the last 100 yards. The filly from Doninga beat Allez France by three-quarters of a length, with five lengths to the next of the 16-strong field. The owner of Allez France, Daniel Wildenstein, claimed that his filly was sent on too soon and those most expected to give Allez France the most trouble, Moulton, Mysterious and Scottish Rifle never lived up to their reputations.

After the Champion Stakes, Hurry Harriet went for the Washington International in the USA but had little chance to show her worth. Her saddle slipped forward in the early stages and the jockey, Jean Cruguet, spent the rest of the race on her withers. The rule there was that the valets saddled the horse, and the trainer was not allowed to take charge of this vital task. Recalls Paddy, 'She was a long way in front at half way, and even after half way. She had a terrible pair of withers and you would need to have the saddle glued to her. The race was won by Dahlia who also won the Irish Guinness Oaks in which Hurry Harriet came third.' At the end of April 1974 Hurry Harriet began to have tendon trouble. A vet came across from England and performed some surgery on her.

Hurry Harriet began running fairly well again, and won races, but it was felt that she was no longer the force she had been. Her only run of the 1974 season came on 2 November when she won the Trigo Stakes at The Curragh, with Walter Swinburn riding. In 1975, again at The Curragh, she won the Ballymoss Stakes, this time with Johnny Roe in the saddle. Her final race in Ireland came on 13 October at the Phoenix Park when she won the Whitehall Stakes, ridden by National Hunt champion, Tommy Carberry. The horse's other tendon subsequently gave out and her racing career was at an end.

Says Paddy, 'A filly like her, with any little injury like that, could not be kept sound.' Hurry Harriet was sent to one of the leading sires of the time, Thatch, at Coolmore Stud. She was brought to America in foal and sold shortly afterwards to the Texas oil magnate Nelson Bunker Hunt, who was a frequent visitor to race meetings in Europe, especially The Curragh. Both Dr Thorpe and Paddy Mullins had met him. Paddy remembers one unusual aspect of the corpulent, teetotal Texan. 'You never saw him without a lollipop at the races.'

Reflecting on the Hurry Harriet saga, Paddy emphasises the role in the mare's success of Ferdie Murphy, who was head lad and stable jockey at the yard for six years in the early 1970s. Says Paddy, 'Ferdie was here in the Hurry Harriet time and he was instrumental in producing the mare to the degree she achieved. He is a trainer in England now. He was a top-class man, brilliant at his work and used to ride over jumps for us. He used to live in the house next door to us. Ferdie's son Paul works here now, and rides out every day. He rode a couple of winners at Liverpool before coming here. He's about 20. Ferdie asked me to take him for a while – he is a grand kid. First thing he rode for me was a point-to-point winner and did it in super style. An older boy Barry is still in England with his father – he also used to be here. I would have to say that much of the credit for the success of Hurry Harriet must go to Ferdie Murphy.' It's a sentiment that is echoed by Paddy's daughter Sandra. 'It's one of the secrets of success for many horses – the way somebody looks after them,' she says. In April 1995 Ferdie Murphy had a win as a trainer at Punchestown, a course where he had also known success as a jockey, when his charge Postage Stamp took the Coleman Tunnelling Handicap Chase.

Paddy points out that Flat racing has changed a great deal since the 1970s, since the days he won quite a few Flat races with Hurry Harriet and other horses. Trainers like himself find it much harder nowadays to get a winner on the Flat. In fact his main complaint about racing nowadays is the virtual exclusion of the small Flat owner from success on racecourses throughout Ireland. Says Paddy, 'There is no remedy for it. The hugely rich owners have come into this country with huge strings of horses and they clean up. What they are after is a win, a bracket for fillies and they come down the country with fillies that have not made it at The Curragh – not necessarily because they are are not good enough but probably because they are not matured in time. And of course they mop up any little races which the ordinary man might have been winning years ago. This is no doubt frightening people away from buying Flat horses. I did not consciously move away from the Flat – I would say I was squeezed away from it, because the big people were dominating it and you just could not win races. The smaller owners just could not compete.'

CHAPTER 7

A Very Irish Coup

Paddy Mullins has always been noted for his ability to place even a lacklustre horse in a race some time in the animal's career that will give the owner at least one win. Back in 1975 he was particularly anxious that a horse called Silver Road would do well in a race, because the owner had come all the way from America to see his horse in action. But the entire exercise was all to end in disarray. For Paddy was not to have known that the race he chose for the horse was to be the target of a massive coup, one of the biggest ever seen in Ireland. It was the coup that was to catapult poker-faced gambler Barney Curley into the big time.

The year was 1975, and Silver Road's owner was Ed Green, a businessman from Palm Springs, Florida, who had made his money from investing in orange futures. Green was just one of the foreign owners from faraway places that the Mullins stable has accumulated over the years. As often happens, he had been introduced to Paddy by other owners of his – in this case Dotsie and Henry Rudkin, who were enjoying very good success with Brendon's Road. Silver Road was competent at his job but not in the same class as Brendon's Road, so, after some intensive study of the racing calendar, Paddy chose an obscure race at Bellewstown which, he reckoned, would be ideal for the horse. There did not seem to be much competition and, with a little bit of luck, the horse might just pick up a win and the owner would return home happy. Unfortunately, as it was to turn out, the race had also attracted the eagle-eyed attention of former Jesuit seminarian Barney Curley who was also on the lookout for the chance to land a 'touch' – but a 'touch' with a difference.

The day dawned, and the Doninga team, along with Ed Green, turned up at Bellewstown. It was 4 August 1975, a fine, sunny day. There's always a great atmosphere at Bellewstown – it's in the middle of the countryside, a bit off the beaten track, and is very much a 'rural' racecourse. It's also one of the oldest racecourses in Ireland. Like The Curragh, it dates back to the seventeenth century. For Green, visiting Bellewstown was a culture shock. The rustic racecourse, set among farmlands and woods and winding country roads, was about as far removed as anyone could imagine from the sophisticated courses he had known back in America, with their top-class restaurants and bars. And, as was to emerge later, the phone facilities at Bellewstown were not the most sophisticated either.

Paddy's son Willy was riding Silver Road that day. Willy had begun his race riding career unexpectedly in November 1973 while still at boarding school. Willy had come home for the weekend when his father told him, out of the blue, in his usual laconic style, that he now had an amateur rider's licence and would be riding next day in a bumper at Fairyhouse. It was Willy's first ride on a racecourse. He had his first win a few months later, on 13 August 1974 when, riding Silver Road, he won the Metal Man Amateur Maiden Hurdle at Tramore. He had had a number of wins since then, and now found himself, at Bellewstown, at the age of 18, trying to 'do the biz' once more on Silver Road, the horse that had given him his first taste of victory on a racecourse.

Silver Road's owner, Ed Green, meanwhile, had got his bets on with the bookies and was eagerly awaiting the thrill of the handicap hurdle race – and, hopefully, the massive buzz an owner gets when he sees his horse thunder in first past the finishing line. The race started and Willy reckoned he was doing well. Then, seemingly from nowhere and to his amazement and dismay, another horse powered past him like a rocket. It was Yellow Sam, who went on to win easily. Unfortunately Silver

Road could not get up to be second and had to be content with third place. Says Willy, 'We were mystified as to how we could have run so well and still been beaten. Of course it all came out in the wash. I can't remember how we found out that there had been this huge gamble, that a coup had taken place and that the single phone line from Bellewstown had been tied up by the people behind the coup.' The sad part was that even if Yellow Sam had not run that day, Silver Road would still not have won the race! Paddy was very annoyed afterwards when some busybody came along and tried to rub salt in Ed Green's wounds by saying, 'Your trainer must not think much of your horse's prospects to run him in a place like Bellewstown.' The remark was grossly unfair to Paddy – and to Bellewstown.

The newspapers were full of the story of the coup over the next few days. High-rolling gambler Barney Curley had carried out one of the boldest and most brilliantly-executed coups in racing history – and it was all entirely legal. Curley's horse Yellow Sam hadn't shown any form in previous outings. Large amounts of money had been laid on the 'nose' by Curley's trusted lieutenants in S. P. offices and the bookies were thwarted in getting the money back to the track, so the horse went off at 20–1 whereas it might otherwise have been returned at odds-on. These were the days before mobile phones and the S.P. bookies could not get through to the track. This was because a large, heavily-built man, a sort of tough-looking man, had occupied the only phone box at Bellewstown having discovered that a relative was seriously ill and once he had the phone in his hand would not relinquish it for anybody. It's reckoned the bookies were 'cleaned' to the tune of at least £250,000.

Ed Green, for his part, took it all in his stride. Paddy and Maureen Mullins were to later spend a holiday at his home in north Palm Beach. Recalls Paddy, 'We used to go to the Canaries on our holidays but Ed would say to us, "Why don't you come to Florida where there is real sun?" So we went over to stay with him. I remember being out this dull, cloudy day, and ended up getting the worst sunburn of my life.' One consolation for Paddy regarding the year 1975 was that it was during that season that he sent out his biggest total of winners to date – a total of 56. Andy Pandy ran up a great sequence of wins on the Flat and over hurdles and then went on to 'chasing, winning the Ulster Bank Novice Chase at Mallow on 13 December. He went on to win three more 'chases in 1976 and was then sold to England, where he was to perform well for Fred Rimell. Prince Tammy, Negrada and Parijatak were also among Paddy's winning horses during 1975. Escott, owned by Lady Elizabeth Byng won a series of 'chases through 1975 and the following year. A successful Flat horse during this period was Roll Up, which took the November Handicap at Leopardstown in November 1975 and was later sold to India.

Meanwhile, Barney Curley, with the money from the Yellow Sam coup and other gambles, was able to set up home in Midleton Park, a Georgian mansion set in almost 380 acres in Co. Westmeath, about 50 miles from Dublin, and formerly the family home of the trainer Cecil Boyd-Rochfort. In 1984 Curley got into trouble with the authorities for raffling off his mansion – but it's thought he may have made up to £500,000 on the operation. He later moved to Newmarket to train and became noted as an outspoken critic of various aspects of the racing and bookmaking scene.

Paddy Mullins has got to know Barney Curley and the two men are on first name terms. 'I have a lot of respect for Barney Curley,' says Paddy. But a high-rolling gambler, Paddy certainly is not. He has seen too many unpredictable things happen in racing to risk big sums with the bookies. When he goes to the races he likes to have a modest bet now and then, but he considers it unlucky to gamble on his own horses. As he says himself, 'I was never a betting man but I would have an interest.' The Mullins stable is not a gambling stable. Referring to betting in general, he says, 'It's really a lottery. If people only realised what can happen to a horse from the time it leaves the parade ring.' He agrees that betting coups do happen from time to time – the Yellow Sam one being a prime example. But he does not believe they happen to the extent people think they do.

He believes it would be very difficult to keep confidential

the kind of information that would enable a coup to take place. If a horse starts showing ability in any stable, it's difficult to keep the information under wraps, he says. 'My experience of it is that any horse that starts showing a little bit of promise, the whole country knows about it before you can say Jack Robinson.' He says that he himself has never been involved in a coup. He did recall one very successful gamble that was organised during the time he was associated with the Kirwan stables in 1953. In the Rathdrum Handicap Hurdle at Leopardstown on 28 February that year, Dress Parade won in comfortable style. The *Irish Field* commented afterwards that 'although Mr J. O'Donoghue's mare was one of the outsiders with the general public, she was by no means neglected by her connections, and some nice wagers were struck at attractively long odds'.

Paddy Mullins has reservations about having big-time gamblers as owners, believing there can be problems with some of them. 'You would be supposed to dish out the information and if a horse wins as often times happens, and the gambling owner is not on it, you will have his friends saying to him, "Weren't you on that? We were." So then you have recriminations. And then some owners will feel they should have been told something when there was really nothing to tell. And the thing will be fuelled by outsiders who come along and say they knew I had it backed or some of my other owners backed it on my recommendation, and the owner himself was left out. That's what happens. Rumours circulate all the time. And people make up stories to an incredible degree. They make them up!'

On one occasion Paddy phoned one of his owners, a keen gambler, to tell him that his horse was running the next day. The horse had been in preparation for the race for quite some time and seemed to have a very good chance. The news that the horse was about to run was greeted with shock and dismay by the gambling owner.

'Sure you can't run him tomorrow,' says the owner.

'Why not?' says Paddy.

'Because I've no money to back him!'

Paddy Mullins has had a large number of owners over the years, and it would be very hard to generalise about them when it came to their attitude towards having a gamble. Mrs Charmian Hill, owner of Dawn Run, the most famous horse over jumps ever trained at Doninga, never seems to have gambled on the mare at all. Another owner, Paddy Kehoe, who had a half share in another very successful jump horse, Grabel, is well-known as a high-rolling punter. Unlike Mrs Hill, whose monetary pay-off from Dawn Run came in the form of prize money, for Paddy Kehoe, the pay-off comes from gambling. 'Prize money doesn't matter,' he says, no doubt with some exaggeration. As a trainer Paddy Mullins does not generally seem to attract the big-time gamblers, as his stable is not regarded as a 'gambling stable'.

But whether he is dealing with owners who gamble in a big way or in a small way, he has learned from experience that a trainer has to be careful what he says to an owner about a horse's chances in a particular race – or even the horse's long-term prospects. Some owners are so eager for good news about their horse that they may be tempted to seize on any throwaway comment by a trainer as an indication that the horse is going to perform far better than the animal's capabilities will allow. As regards a horse's long-term future, Paddy says he will quite often have a plan for the horse mapped out but so many things can go wrong that he will sometimes be reluctant to commit himself too far in advance to an owner regarding such a plan.

When a race is taking place that day or the following day, he has a dread of saying something that will be misinterpreted by an owner, leading him to splurge with the bookies when he really should be cautious. He recalls one incident involving Lock Diamond, one of his good Flat horses from the late 1960s. The horse had been bred by a local farmer, the late Des Connolly who failed to sell him as a yearling. Mr Connolly approached Paddy and asked him to put the horse in training. Paddy advised him that the horse would be better off with one of the Flat trainers on The Curragh but Mr Connolly insisted that he wanted the animal trained at Doninga. Against his better judgement, Paddy took the horse into training and he began showing some promise as a two-year-old. It was decided then to run him in his first race at Limerick Junction on 16 May 1968, the horse's birthday.

Paddy believes now he must have given some unintended signal to Des Connolly that led to him being super-confident about the horse's chances on the day. For after the trainer arrived at the racecourse he found, to his dismay, that there was a 'tip' out for Lock Diamond. The owner had built up his hopes, even though Paddy had never wanted to give him the impression that the horse had a good chance. The bookies were giving good odds at first about Lock Diamond, but the odds tightened up as the money, following the tip, flowed onto the horse. There was at least one sceptic on the day who did not fancy Lock Diamond's chances. Paddy recalls how the late Jimmy Eddery, father of the jockey Pat Eddery, remarked that Paddy Mullins might be a good trainer over jumps but there was no way he'd win a Flat race like this.

A very young jockey, Paddy Neill, was riding Lock Diamond on the day and the duo were to give the trainer the surprise of his life – and happily, a pleasant surprise. Paddy recalls, 'The horse just jumped out of the gate and bolted in. Lock Diamond's first ever race, and he won it in fine style. Des Connolly was walking on air. Fellows had been laughing at him but he had the last laugh. It certainly came as a very pleasant surprise to me when he won. He was a very decent horse afterwards, going on to win three more races on the Flat before winning his maiden hurdle at Navan in 1970 and then going on to win over fences, winning the Buttevant Chase at Mallow. Des never let me forget how sorry I would have been if he had not persuaded me to take the horse and in the final analysis he was right.' Anybody who picked up Des Connolly's tip that day and backed with the bookies did well. But the incident reinforced Paddy's caution in what he says to owners – or anyone else – about a horse's prospects. In this particular instance, however, it was a case of all's well that ends well.

When Paddy was at a loose end at a race meeting, he would always like to have a look at the odds being offered by the bookies with a view to having a minor wager. It was something to do to pass the time if, say, he did not have a runner until the last race of the day. But he found over the years that too many people were following him around trying to check out what he was backing. He says, 'I would have the occasional bet in a small way. I love having a tenner or a fiver or a score on a horse – but not any of my own. And people think that I back winners, so much so that at times, they would be tailing me around at the races if they saw me moving towards the bookmakers. It's stupid in the extreme. I have more or less given it up for that reason. It has happened that I would turn around after putting on a bet and see a small crowd disperse behind me. They would have been observing what I was backing. I remember this Dublin bookie said to me one day in Gowran Park as I was passing by, "You have as many followers as Jesus Christ." They have great wit, some of these Dublin lads. But the stupidity of it. When they see you in the parade ring they think you are on the inside track.'

In order not to have punters following him around at the racecourse, he began using a friend to put on the bets for him. Unfortunately some of the punters sussed out what was happening and began following the friend around instead. Paddy recalls, 'The man who used to place the bets for me was Tom Brown – his nickname was Gilligan. I happened to fall into his acquaintance one very warm day at the races in Ballinrobe. There was a big crowd in the restaurant and I wanted a quick snack and he stood up and gave me a place to sit down. He was a nice sort of man and as honest as they come. He would put on a bet for me and say, "Keep your hand in your pocket – you can pay me if it loses." He had a mini-cab and taxi business in Portlaoise and we would meet at the races and talk about horses and what we fancied. He died of cancer a couple of years ago. What I would know about the betting and the tips would be minimal, but Gilligan was able to fill in all the gaps because he was floating around. He was able to assimilate all the knowledge and come to me with so much information – wherever it used to emanate from. I could not believe what some of these fellows like Gilligan would pick up. And I can honestly say that when I was friendly with him at race meetings, it was the only time I backed winners.'

Doping is, of course, one activity that can upset the best-laid plans of punters and trainers. While doping is not common, Paddy strongly suspects that, over the years, a dope gang got to two of his horses. He emphasises that the suspected incidents of doping occurred away from his yard, while the horses were at different racecourses, and that no blame of any kind can be applied to anybody who ever worked at his stable. He knows the people he has employed over the years would be vigilant in preventing strangers gaining access to the horses under suspicious circumstances. But it is impossible to guard horses around the clock all the time, as if you were guarding an American president. He recalls how, on one occasion, a horse bore all the tell-tale signs of having been doped with a particular drug. But traces of this drug disappear very quickly from a horse's system. Paddy called in a vet to examine the horse, but if the horse had been doped, there was no trace of the drug in the animal's bloodstream. However, doping is not at the forefront of his mind when Paddy exercises caution in what he says to owners about their horses. For all kinds of innocent reasons, a horse can fail to perform up to expectations, and he never wants to build up an owner's hopes unreasonably. It's an area where a delicate touch is required.

Also requiring a delicate touch is the whole area of buying and selling horses. Of course if a trainer has a horse for sale, he can put the animal into the next sales at Goff's or Tattersall's and take what price it fetches. But if he doesn't want to wait until the sales, and wants a more immediate, or more private transaction, he can use one of the go-betweens who specialise in such matters. A go-between can operate on an agreed commission basis – or he can simply get the buyer his asking price and then make his own profit by selling to the purchaser for a bigger sum. In the latter case, the intermediary's rake-off can be sizeable, and while the deal is in progress he will usually be careful not to reveal the identity of the potential purchaser, in case the seller decides to cut out the middleman.

Paddy recalls a case where an English trainer remarked that he was not satisfied with a horse, considering him bad value for the £30,000 that had been paid for him. Paddy himself was aware that the seller had only received £20,000. In this case, it became clear that the go-between had pocketed a very considerable slice of the action. There was nothing illegal about this, nor, in the world of horse dealing, was there considered to be anything unethical about it either. It was just the way the system worked.

Paddy is very philosophical about the cut that a go-between can get from a deal. He says, 'I have seen people who set themselves up against anything going out of the purchase price – they want everything to go back into the seller's pocket. But personally I believe that people should never make a big issue of it. If you do kick up a fuss, the word will get around, and these fellows who do the deals will be reluctant to get involved with you again. They won't go near somebody who doesn't want them to get their cut, and such a person can end up not being able to sell a horse. The people who do these deals are very professional at the job. They are the ones who have the buyers. They don't usually operate from offices, and they mostly work over the phone. I suppose you could call them freelance agents. They ferret around and get the information, and find out who has the money and wants to buy a horse, and they also find out who wants to sell. If one of these lads gets in touch with you, the first thing he'll ask is, "Is the horse for sale? And if so, for how much?"

'They are quite useful. Unless I was going to put a horse into a sale, if I wanted to sell, I would use one of these men. I need only say to certain people that there is a horse that can be bought, and by God they will start beavering away. I would not necessarily approach them directly. I might tell Tony or Willy or somebody else and let it filter around that way. If a hint gets around that a horse, a decent sort of horse, can be bought, they will quickly get going. The agent wouldn't call in person to the stable here – it would not be as open as that. It would be done over the phone mostly. Some of these fellows are brilliant at doing deals. The late Harry O'Neill, a big gambler in his day from Waterford, was very good at it. If you had a horse to sell, he had a buyer. He would travel to London where he had very good contacts, especially among the Jewish community, and he knew the people who had money and were prepared to spend it on a horse.'

Of course there are times when a good horse will attract offers to buy, frequently from England, and there is no need for a middleman. Very often a potential buyer will ask his trainer to check out the horse. Over the years, Paddy has had a number of well-known English trainers arrive at his yard to see a horse before a deal is done. Among them have been Nicky Henderson, David Nicholson and Capt. Tim Forster. Nowadays point-to-point horses are a major source of supply for people who want to buy racehorses. Says Paddy Mullins, 'I know of a point-to-point horse that was sold for £40,000, and that would not be the dearest either. A good point-to-point horse can go for over £50,000 or even £70,000. Merry Gale, who started out as a point-to-point horse and went on to become a very good 'chaser, winning the Martell Cup Chase at Aintree in 1995, started the trend. When people buy a good point-to-point horse, they feel they are getting a guarantee that the horse can jump.'

CHAPTER 8

Like Father . . .

It soon became apparent to Paddy Mullins in the late 1960s and early 1970s that all his children wanted to make their living from horses. He had mixed feelings about this. He was afraid there would not be enough opportunities for them. He tried to suggest other career paths, other professions to them. But nothing he could say or do could persuade them to do other than opt for a career to do with horses. It was as if it was in the blood. All five children went away to boarding school for their secondary education. Sandra was at the Sacred Heart convent in Roscrea, while Willy, George and Tony went to the Mount St Joseph school, also in Roscrea, run by the Cistercian monks. Tom went to Newtown School, Waterford. And when they left school, all five knew exactly what they wanted to do.

Says Paddy, with a slight note of exasperation in his voice, 'The entire family followed me into the racing business – I could not get them to do anything else. I wanted them to do something else. I thought there was not room in it for them all. When some of the boys were at school in Roscrea I preached to them every time I got a chance, "Go on and do something else." I might as well have been talking to the table. But they're all doing well for themselves. Touch wood.'

All five children began to ride in races during the 1970s, and they have all ridden winners. Tony and Willy are now well-known trainers. Tony is based beside Gowran Park racecourse, while Willy trains and lives at a farm in Closutton, about four miles from Doninga, in the Leighlinbridge area of Co. Carlow. The farm was originally bought by Paddy in 1973 as his business expanded. George, who has ridden a number of winners since his first win with a horse called Cheated at Roscommon on 19 July 1977, also has a house at Closutton. From there he runs a horse transport business, arranging for the transport of horses all over the world, and also a business providing paper bedding for stables. He also rears and deals in horses.

Tom, whose first winner was Solar Cottage, at Wexford in 1980, lives in Kilkenny but works from the stables at Doninga, where he is assistant trainer to his father. He plans to build a house near the yard. He also rears and deals in horses and, of course, has ridden many winners as an amateur for his father over the years. He has been schooling horses over jumps from the age of nine, having started his riding career on ponies almost as soon as he could walk. Sandra, whose first winner was in 1980 at Tralee has a stud farm at Dungarvan, Co. Kilkenny, a few miles from the Mullins yard. She went on to ride other winners. Mrs Maureen Mullins followed the example of her children by riding a winner on Razzo Forte in the annual Flat race for trainers' wives and daughters at Gowran Park in 1982. The horse went on to win his next two races, ridden by David Parnell and Joanna Morgan.

Maureen remembers her win on Razzo Forte for another reason – it was the year she and Paddy went on the holiday of a lifetime to Kenya. Through Buster Parnell and other contacts they met some leading trainers in that country, some of whom had Irish connections. She remembers visiting one training establishment where the gallops were in a circle around the trainer's house – presumably so he could watch his charges at work without leaving the comfort of his verandah. Maureen and Paddy went to the races while they were in Kenya. It was one of the farthest flung places they had ever gone to attend a race meeting and the African track certainly made a change from the familiar surroundings of the likes of Gowran Park.

All five children of Paddy and Maureen Mullins have

married spouses connected with horses or racing. Tony's wife Mags, a well-known jockey, has won quite a few races, while Willy's wife Jackie was champion woman jockey for the 1994–95 season, riding 18 winners. Born in England of medical doctor parents, Jackie has a law degree. Her Irish mother has relatives in the stud farm business in Ireland. George's wife Brigid is a member of the Phelan family near Kilmacthomas who are deeply involved with horses, and Tom's wife Helen comes from a Gowran family who have been involved in the business of horses for generations. Her showjumping sister Marion Hughes has become very well known in the sport in Ireland and abroad. Sandra's husband Peter McCarthy, a son of the singer Veronica Dunne, is a Dublin businessman and was also a skilled amateur rider. He rode his first winner at Tramore, on 18 August 1977 and followed it up with another win at Bellewstown six days later.

In the mid-1970s there was yet another reminder, as if one were needed, of the Mullins family's link with horses when Negrada, belonging to Paddy's brother Luke, won the Guinness Hurdle. The date was 29 July 1976 and it was Paddy's first win in this event at the Galway Festival, and Luke, having retired from the army as a captain, was manager of Galway racecourse, scene of the victory. Paddy recalls how Luke had to bow out from a group of friends in the bar saying, 'You will have to excuse me – as manager of the racecourse I have to go to the parade ring to organise a presentation to myself.' Earlier in the year, Negrada had won hurdle races at Leopardstown and Dundalk, and had also won on the Flat when, ridden by Joanna Morgan, he took the Melitta Stakes at The Curragh.

One of the other horses scoring multiple wins for the stable that year was Prince Tammy, owned by Kevin O'Donnell, a farmer from Gowran and a director of Gowran Park racecourse. Another one of the winners from the yard that year was Kilcoo Lad, owned by local man Paddy Kehoe (not to be confused with the Paddy Kehoe who was co-owner of Grabel). Paddy remembers Mr Kehoe, who died in 1995, as an old friend and a great sportsman. 'Paddy Kehoe used to ride in point-to-points and in races during my time. I remember a hunter's chase over banks at Fairyhouse one day and I thought I would beat him. Paddy and I landed together at the last and I was convinced I would win and to my surprise he started kicking on and I could not get him. I only realised when we were pulling up that the reason he was getting such results was that he had a fine pair of sharp spurs on. The horse he was riding was a tough sort of animal. Of course the use of any kind of spurs is now ruled out.' The year 1976 closed with a new record number of winners for the stable, a total of 59.

Counsel Cottage, owned by Lady Elizabeth Byng, had made his debut during 1976, when Willy Mullins rode him to victory in a bumper at Naas, the Halvestown Plate. Counsel Cottage was, of course, bred by Lady Elizabeth herself. Paddy Mullins recalls that he was out of a mare that had also been in training at Doninga. 'The mare was as slow, as near useless as you could find,' says Paddy. 'We ran her in point-to-points and then she got injured. She was sent home to Lady Elizabeth's estate in Hertfordshire and went to stud and bred Counsel Cottage. For such a lacklustre mare to breed such a good horse only goes to show that when it comes to racehorses, there is no such thing as certainty.'

After his initial bumper win, Counsel Cottage made steady progress in his racing career. He had a win in the Sandymount Hurdle at Leopardstown in November 1976, and notched up a series of seconds in other events during 1976 and into 1977. Paddy was impressed by the horse and, in consultation with Lady Elizabeth, decided to let him have a run in the Sun Alliance Hurdle at Cheltenham. There were 26 runners in the race and Sean Treacy settled Counsel Cottage in at the rear for the early stages, with John Francome on the favourite, The Dealer, making the early running. At half-way, Treacy moved Counsel Cottage up as Master Smudge and Chinrullah had taken over from The Dealer. With seven to jump, The Dealer had again taken over and Counsel Cottage moved through the field to challenge. Coming to the last Treacy took Counsel Cottage into the lead and despite drifting to the right held on well up the hill to win from Master Smudge who had come with a late run and The Dealer, with Chinrullah in fourth.

Lady Elizabeth had arrived at Cheltenham that day carrying a shopping bag which she guarded like the Crown jewels. When Counsel Cottage won, a jubilant Lady Elizabeth hurried to lead him in to the winner's enclosure – still carrying the shopping bag. Maureen Mullins had offered to take the bag but Lady Elizabeth adamantly refused to hand it over. As they followed her into the enclosure, Lady Elizabeth's son remarked to Maureen that she should have taken the shopping bag from his mother. Maureen replied, 'I tried, but there was no way she would hand it over.' After the presentation, the mystery of the shopping bag was solved – it was packed with cash. Obviously confident of victory, Lady Elizabeth had prepared extremely generous presents for all those connected with the horse. The shopping bag contained several envelopes, each crammed with crisp, new sterling notes. There were presents for Paddy, the jockey, the head lad Jim Treacy, father of Paddy's present jockey Tommy (T.P.) Treacy, and also money to buy a crate of champagne for the celebrations. Paddy remembers Lady Elizabeth with particular affection, as a real individual who always had her own unique way of doing things. He still has a photo of Lady Elizabeth leading in her horse at Cheltenham – and carrying her shopping bag.

Lady Elizabeth was overjoyed at Counsel Cottage's performance and Paddy also confessed himself to being very pleased indeed to notch up another win at Cheltenham. There had been an interval of close on a decade since Paddy's previous festival win, when Herring Gull took the Champion Novices Chase in 1968. Oddly enough, Counsel Cottage failed to reproduce his Cheltenham form during the remainder of 1977, his best achievements being a second at Punchestown on 26 April and another second at Fairyhouse on 23 November. His form improved the following year when his results from ten outings included five wins and three seconds. Counsel Cottage developed leg trouble and missed the 1979 season but came back with a bang in 1980 and won three 'chases at

Punchestown, Naas and Fairyhouse. He also made a foray into France, coming third in the Prix des Drags in Auteuil. The year 1977 would also be remembered by Lady Elizabeth for another reason. Another of her horses at the Doninga stable, Billy's Cottage, had his first win during that year when, ridden by Willy Mullins, he won the Moyode Plate at Galway. Billy's Cottage, bred by Lady Elizabeth, went on to win three more hurdle races that year. Paddy reflects that Lady Elizabeth never sent him a horse who didn't win.

One of the big events for Paddy and Maureen Mullins during the 1970s from a family point of view, was the wedding, in 1978, of their daughter Sandra. She was the first of the Mullins children to tie the knot. The white wedding was held at Paulstown church, and among the guests were two stewards of the Turf Club, Denis McCarthy, an uncle of the groom, and the late Major Victor McCalmont. Some of Paddy's owners were there too, including Tom Nicholson and Tony Onions, both of whom had been with him since the 1950s, and the redoubtable Lady Elizabeth Byng. Tony Onions was having considerable success at this period with his Mullins-trained horse Rosie O'Grady.

For much of the decade of the 1970s, the yearly tally of winners for the Doninga stable showed a gradual rise, and 1978 was one of the most successful years of all, with a total of 74 winners. The following year, 1979, saw the number of winners totalling 54 and it also saw three of the Mullins brothers riding winners. Tony was getting his riding career under way in fine fashion. After his first win on Pearlstone in an August bumper at Tramore, he was to notch up six more winners that year, including a win in his first hurdle race when he rode his mother's horse, Inarticulate, to victory in the Amateur Handicap Hurdle at Thurles. Willy also rode winners, and George had a total of three, including one on Victor's Barge in the Amateur Handicap Hurdle at Galway. Victor's Barge turned out to be quite a good horse, winning five hurdle races and a novice 'chase the following year.

An event that was later to prove very significant for the Mullins stable happened during the decade of the 1970s – the formidable Mrs Charmian Hill began to send her horses for training to Doninga, and one of these, in the 1980s, was to be the legendary Dawn Run. Mrs Hill had horses previously with trainer Willy O'Grady but when he died she looked for a stable that would be convenient to her own Waterford home and selected the Mullins yard.

In Mrs Hill, Paddy was not just taking on an owner, but a jockey as well. When it came to women riding in races, Mrs Hill was a true pioneer. On 8 December 1979 she rode her own horse, the Mullins-trained Yes Man to victory in the Ulster Bank Novice Chase at Clonmel, becoming the first woman in Irish racing to win on the Flat, over hurdles and in a 'chase – no mean achievement. Earlier that year Mrs Hill, who had begun race riding at the quite late age of 40, had won hurdle races riding Yes Man at Listowel and Tramore. But she was to suffer terrible injuries in November 1980 when Yes Man fell at Thurles. The horse died of a broken neck and Mrs Hill spent four months at the National Rehabilitation Centre. She emerged weighing just six stone. But the experience was not to put her off either horses or riding in races.

The following year, in the company of the retired groom Jack Evoy who helped her with horses, she went to the Ballsbridge Sales and bought a mare that had been bred by Mr John Riordan, of Rathcormac, Co. Cork. Dawn Run almost did not survive her first few days on earth. Her dam, Twilight Slave, was sickly, so Mr Riordan's wife Prudence fed the foal on glucose and Complan for weeks until the mother was strong enough to suckle her offspring. When Mrs Hill first saw Dawn Run, it was almost as if she was hit by a bolt of lightning. It was a question of love at first sight. Mrs Hill just knew that this was the one for her. Mrs Hill's daughter Penny was rising early at the time to train for a marathon, so the new mare was called Dawn Run. The mare was to be sent to Paddy Mullins for training and the rest, as they say, is history.

In the late 1970s Paddy gained another remarkable woman as a client. This was the American-born Nancy, Lady Dunraven, of Adare Manor, Co. Limerick. She sent a horse for training to

Paddy called Hav' A Heart. The late Lady Dunraven was a member of a leading Irish aristocratic family and loved racing. Meanwhile, the nature of Paddy's clientele had been changing gradually during the 1970s, according to his son Willy. He reckons that in the old days, many of the owners were farmers or landed gentry. In the 1970s, they noticed that many of the owners were coming from the cities, and were involved in business or the professions, not the land. 'It was as if the money had left the country and was in the towns and cities,' says Willy.

* * *

Around the end of the 1970s, Paddy renewed his professional links with French racing. The French were worried about the increasing popularity of trotting races and wanted to boost interest in jump racing by attracting horses from abroad. And so they invited trainers from various countries to France in an effort to interest them in sending horses to race there. Paddy, who had had successes in Paris with Nor and Herring Gull in 1970, was one of the Irish trainers who accepted the invitation to France.

Paddy made good use of his visit to France, studying French racing carefully. Some time afterwards, he brought out four horses to race in Auteuil, among them Pearlstone and Luska. The trip was subsidised by the French racing authorities, who gave the Doninga trainer the use of part of a trainer's yard near Auteuil. He did not have a winner, but the horses ran respectably and he felt he was learning all the time. Luska, ridden by T. V. Finn, took part in the Prix Millionaire at Auteuil but finished a long way behind Mon Filleul. The horse, ridden by J. P. Harty, also ran in the 'Grand Steep' but without success. However, ridden by J. P. Delaporte, Luska managed a respectable fifth place in the Prix des Drags.

Says Paddy, 'From my trips to France, I got the hang of French schooling and French jumps. I was the only Irish trainer to bring horses over to France in the aftermath of that trainers' trip. Nobody said it to me at the time, but I'm sure some people thought I was mad. But it all paid off later, when Dawn Run won in Paris.'

Meanwhile in 1980, Paddy made another expedition to France, this time with Counsel Cottage. He had consulted with Lady Elizabeth Byng, and was tempted to see if he could pull off a win in Paris with Counsel Cottage as he had done with Herring Gull ten years previously. Paddy and Maureen stayed in the same small hotel in Chantilly where they had stayed during the Herring Gull trip a decade before. They have very happy memories of the hotel, the food, the ambience and the friendly owner, a M. Moulins, who used to insist that he and Paddy shared the same surname.

Assisting Paddy in Paris on this trip was the veteran English jockey, Martin Blackshaw, who had gone to train in France. Some years previously Blackshaw had been badly injured in a fall from a horse in France which resulted in an extended stay in hospital. Blackshaw was worried about the hospital bills but was told by the hospital authorities that they were being paid by a mystery benefactor. Blackshaw afterwards found that it was his old racing rival Lester Piggott who had come to his aid. Blackshaw helped with the schooling of Counsel Cottage over the French jumps, and went on to ride the horse in the Grand Steeplechase de Paris on 29 June. Unfortunately, Blackshaw had to pull up the horse. There was a better result for the connections shortly afterwards, when Blackshaw rode Counsel Cottage into third place in the Prix des Drags, the 'consolation race' for the 'Grand Steep'. Maureen Mullins in particular has happy memories of Counsel Cottage getting a place in the prestigious Auteuil event. It reminded her of Stan Mellor's great performance in the same race a decade earlier.

Lady Elizabeth was ill at the time and was unable to travel to Paris for the race. Martin Blackshaw was to die tragically in a car crash some time later, while driving early one morning to the gallops where he exercised his horses. Meanwhile Counsel Cottage resumed racing in Ireland but was badly injured at Fairyhouse. Recalls Paddy, 'He cut his tendon right across and should have been put down but Lady Elizabeth brought him home to Hertfordshire, and he lived to a ripe old age. She would keep horses forever.'

* * *

The 1980 season opened with a win for a horse owned by Mrs Hill. Her Kilbricken Money, ridden by J. P. Byrne gave Paddy his first winner when taking a handicap chase at Tramore on 31 January. The Goresbridge stable went on to send out a total of 49 winners during the year and without doubt the one that gave Paddy most pleasure came at Tralee on 3 September when his daughter Sandra rode her first winner under Rules. She rode I'm Ready to victory in the Ulster Bank ladies' race held during the annual Rose of Tralee festival. I'm Ready went on to give Paddy his first Irish Cambridgeshire success ten days later at The Curragh, ridden by an apprentice, Pat Shanahan.

Sandra's first ride in a race was on Self Defence at Leopardstown some time in the 1970s. She says ruefully that she was the last of Paddy's offspring to ride a winner. 'I could not believe it when I won at Tralee. I was years waiting.' The fact that it was a ladies' race was a big help to her in winning because of the weights, she reckons. She was very light and normally, riding in bumpers, she had to carry so much lead that she could hardly feel the horse under her. But in the ladies' race she did not have to carry as much lead. So what was her father's reaction when she won? 'He didn't say anything,' says Sandra. However, Paddy did remark to his wife Maureen, with obvious satisfaction, 'Well, Sandra has done now what she wanted to do.' Maureen bred and owned I'm Ready, and the horse was later sold to America. Sandra was different from her brothers in that, for part of her life at least, she worked or studied in areas that had nothing to do with horses. She worked in Dublin for Guinness for a time after leaving school and also travelled abroad. After she married, Sandra studied at University College Dublin, taking out a BA degree in History and German. But the call of the horses was always there and her stud farm now keeps her busy.

* * *

Luska was one of the big achievers for the Mullins stable in 1981. He won the Irish Grand National that year and became known among the lads in the yard at Doninga as the Guinness-drinking horse, his owner deciding that a drop of the black stuff would help to build up his strength and would be good for his health. It was an excuse that human imbibers of the brew had been using in Ireland for generations. Of course, in the case of Luska, the health argument wasn't just a cover for hitting the hard stuff. There is a school of thought that Guinness really is good for horses, because of the yeast content. Paddy Mullins subscribes to this view and recalls how one of his owners, a publican, used to bring slops to the yard for his horse. Paddy points out, however, that stout would normally be a costly addition to an animal's feed. While horses do not have to worry about the price of a pint, the owners do.

Luska was owned by John Brophy, a second cousin of Paddy Mullins. And it was after his Grand National win that Brophy decided on that special tonic for the horse. John Clarke, who was a lad in the yard at the time, and who was later to become famous as Dawn Run's groom, remembers Luska's stout-swilling days extremely well. 'Crates of Guinness would come down to the yard and we would empty the bottles into Luska's feed bucket,' says John. 'We were afraid at first that the horse would be drunk going around the gallops but it turned out that Luska could handle his liquor well. After about seven weeks the Guinness stopped coming.'

John Brophy had degrees in agriculture and had worked in the earlier part of his career for the Department of Agriculture. He knew a lot about horses and used to have horses in training with the late Paddy Murphy in Kilcullen, Co. Kildare. After buying a farm in Co. Kilkenny, Brophy sent Paddy a couple of horses to train during the 1970s. Luska, who was among the horses brought out to Auteuil in the late 1970s by Paddy Mullins, began winning races during 1980, with two of Paddy's sons, Willy and George, riding the horse to victory. Despite a disappointing showing at the Cheltenham Festival in 1981, it was decided to enter him for the Irish Grand National, to be held on the opening day of the Fairyhouse Easter festival on 21 April that year. Entering the last mile, the leader was Royal Stuart and he was joined by Luska, with Bective Road, Last Suspect and Pillar Brae well in contention. At the fifth last fence, Royal Stuart made a mistake, as did Last Suspect, allowing Luska to move up right behind the leader, Royal Stuart. Then Royal Stuart made another mistake, leaving Luska, ridden by Tommy Finn, to battle it out with Pillar Brae, the mount of Ted Walsh. Luska won in fine style, beating Pillar Brae by a length, with Last Suspect 15 lengths behind in third place. Luska's victory gave the stable its fourth win in the Irish Grand National. Luska also took part in the Aintree Grand National, but without success.

One of Paddy's winners during the 1981 season was Footstick, who won a bumper at Naas in July and a maiden hurdle at Tramore in August. Footstick was to accompany Paddy on one of his more unusual trips abroad, when the horse was entered for the Norwegian Grand National in Oslo in September 1984. Paddy had been invited to take part and decided to have a go with Footstick, a horse that had been owned by his late brother Jim. The jockey was Jim's son Seamus who was later to ride Boraceva to victory in the National Hunt Chase at the 1989 Cheltenham Festival. Footstick failed to shine on the day, coming eighth in the race.

Another Mullins horse that made her debut in the winner's enclosure during the 1981 season was Girl In Blue. The late David Parnell rode her to victory in the Writers Week Flat race at Listowel on 22 September. Owned and bred by Maureen Mullins, the mare was to go on to win the Irish Lincolnshire in 1984. Although the winning strike rate dropped to 41 for the 1981 season another promising recruit appeared on the scene when Hazy Dawn, who was to add considerably to the stable's reputation, won her bumper at Clonmel on 8 December ridden by Willy Mullins. She closed the season in style when taking the Dunsany Novice Chase at Navan on 21 December in the hands of T. V. Finn, showing promise of much better things to come.

CHAPTER 9

The Arabs Come to Doninga

Paddy Mullins acquired a client in the 1980s who was definitely out of the ordinary – an Arab billionaire from the unreal world of oil-rich Saudi royalty. Mahmoud Fustok, a brother-in-law of the fabulously wealthy Crown Prince Abdullah of Saudi Arabia, had dealings with Paddy for a period in the 1980s. He sent three horses to be trained at Doninga and he also introduced Paddy to a number of jetsetters from his own exotic world, including Egyptian-born movie star Omar Sharif, whom Paddy remembers as 'a very nice fellow'. It all happened through a wealthy Irish client whom Paddy had at the time. This client, who liked to keep a low profile, had quite a good horse at Doninga, and had very good political and business connections in Ireland and abroad. It was he who introduced Mahmoud Fustok to Paddy.

Fustok was of Palestinian origin but had been living in Saudi Arabia for many years, where his connections were of the highest. His sister was married to Crown Prince Abdullah, one of the most powerful men in the oil-rich desert kingdom. Fustok owned some very good racehorses, as well as the top-class Buckram Oak stud farm at Lexington, Kentucky, which is one of the leading stud farms in America, and he also owned a racing stable at Chantilly, France. One of the horses Fustok had in training with Paddy was Regal Nilke, who was sent to Doninga as a yearling. Regal Nilke developed leg trouble, and Fustok did not want to keep him. He was acquired by Paddy and ultimately went on to win races.

One of the main services that Paddy supplied to Fustok was to take on as a trainee at the yard the teenage son of one of Fustok's old family friends. The teenager was Mohammed Mubarak, who was later to go on to train for Fustok in Newmarket and in America. Over the past few years he has trained some very good winners, including some Group 1 winners. Mohammed was not exactly like the average lad in the average Irish racing establishment. He drove a brand-new BMW and always appeared to have plenty of money. Maureen Mullins remembers, with amusement, going to call him one morning while he was still in bed to tell him that the veterinary surgeon had arrived and was treating one of the horses. She suggested it might be useful for Mohammed to see how the vet worked. Mohammed peeped out from under the bed clothes and declared, 'It's all right, Mrs Mullins, when I begin training myself, I will have my own resident vet.' Says Maureen, 'He wasn't telling a word of a lie – he did indeed have his own resident vet at his stable in later years!'

Mohammed had grown up in Beirut as it was being torn apart by civil strife during the 1970s. He and his family stayed on amid the danger, hoping that the fighting would stop. But after a couple of years of warfare they finally tired of sheltering in basements from bombs and shells and decided to leave the most dangerous city in the world and move to England. His family had close ties to the Fustok family and so it was natural that Mahmoud Fustok would look after the young son of the Mubarak family. Fustok, for his part, was already a highly successful owner before establishing a link with Paddy Mullins. In 1980 his filly Anifa, ridden by former French champion jockey Alfred Gibert, won the $300,000 Turf Classic at Aquaduct, near New York. The young Mohammed Mubarak got on very well with everyone at the yard in Doninga, and he loved being in Ireland. The tranquillity of the Co. Kilkenny countryside was quite a change from battle-scarred Beirut. Maureen Mullins recalls just one occasion on which he became angry. It was when one of the stable lads turned up for work wearing a jacket bearing what Mohammed thought was a Zionist symbol!

Mohammed Mubarak himself has very happy memories of his time in Doninga. He says it was there, from Paddy Mullins, that he acquired the knowledge that forms a basis for the career that he pursues today in America – a career as trainer for Mahmoud Fustok. He recalls, 'I spent two periods at the Mullins yard in the 1980s, each of about eight months. I learned an awful lot from Paddy. It was my first real experience of living and working at a racing stable. I had been, on and off, to the Fustok stables at Chantilly during my holidays. But at Doninga it was really different. All Paddy's sons were there – Willy, George, Tony and Tom. I lived in the house with them and worked with them. There was no distinction between us. I was just one of the boys.

'It was at Paddy's yard that I learned to ride. I did all the things you do at a stable. I rode out, cleaned out stables and cleaned horses. There was no set pattern. There was something different to do every day. George had trucks and he would transport horses and I used to travel a lot with George when he would be moving foals, yearlings and horses around. I also have some very good memories of going to Loughlin's pub in Gowran. It was my first experience of a pub.'

At one stage Fustok took over the leading hotel in the French resort of Deauville, the Hotel Royale, to entertain his friends during the races there. He brought Paddy and Maureen Mullins out to Deauville as his guests for ten days. Mohammed went with them. Paddy recalls how there was supposed to be a limousine waiting for them when they arrived at the airport in Paris, but when they could not find it, Mohammed immediately ordered a taxi to take them to Deauville. The taxi fare came to about £150. Omar Sharif, an old friend of Fustok's, was one of the guests at the Hotel Royale. Says Paddy, 'I met Sharif. He's a lovely man. Great gambler. Loved to play backgammon.' Maureen recalls that when they would be returning late in the evening to the hotel, they would see Sharif settling down to a game of backgammon that could go on all night. Fustok also was a 'night person'. Says Paddy, 'He would love to stay up until the early hours, just talking to people – mostly about horses. He would be asking me all kinds of questions about horses and racing.'

During this trip Paddy met the parents of Mohammed Mubarak. The lad's father was grateful to Paddy for looking after his son and embraced the Doninga man. Paddy has a vivid memory of the man's stubbly beard brushing against his face. But they could not actually say anything to each other because they did not have a language in common. Paddy's impression was that the Mubaraks had a very special relationship with the Fustok family.

Some of the wealthy Arab men who gathered at the Hotel Royale also brought their wives but in line with Middle East custom, the wives kept a very low profile. Maureen used to meet the women on the stairs. They told her they had to stay in the background. The wealth of Mahmoud Fustok was very apparent. Paddy recalls, 'While we were in Deauville, somebody told Fustok that our son George was very friendly with Mohammed Mubarak, and Fustok immediately, at his own expense, made arrangements to have George brought over from Ireland to join us in the hotel.'

Mohammed Mubarak was to go on to become a trainer at the Fustok yard in Newmarket. He was quite successful, recording a number of good wins in events such as the Yorkshire Oaks, the Royal Lodge at Ascot and the Mill Reef Stakes at Goodwood. Among the better horses he trained were Greenline Express and Magnificent Star. He returned to Beirut a few years ago to get married, and for some years now has been training for Mahmoud Fustok at various stables in America. He works much of the time at stables near Miami, no doubt still putting into practice some of the lessons he learned from Paddy Mullins many years ago.

* * *

When the owner of the Paddy Mullins-trained Hazy Dawn won the National Hunt four mile 'chase in Cheltenham in 1982, he marked his euphoria in a unique way. To the great delight of the

Irish crowd, he sang 'Danny Boy' in the unsaddling enclosure. There was no better man to sing on that occasion, for the owner in question was Roly Daniels, one of Ireland's leading country singers. Paddy Mullins himself was delighted in a special way about the marvellous win, for the rider was his own son Willy. He had had two previous winners at the festival, Herring Gull in 1968 and Counsel Cottage in 1977. But it was the first time he had had a winner at Cheltenham ridden by a member of his own family.

The win was also special in a particular way for Willy, as it was his first ride at the festival, and to have a win on his first outing at Cheltenham was something to remember. He had been working for trainer Jim Bolger at the time but there was no problem about taking the mount for his father. Willy says, 'I thought the day I rode Hazy Dawn to win at Cheltenham struck a chord with my father. After all, he had trained the winner himself and his own son had ridden it. I felt on the day it was something special for him. He doesn't really show excitement, but I knew on the day that he was really pleased, even though he did not say very much.' Paddy's son-in-law Peter McCarthy says that this was the only occasion on which he detected an emotional reaction by the trainer following a win.

Hazy Dawn had been in training with Pat Hughes, who trains just a couple of miles away from the Mullins stable. Roly Daniels's brother-in-law Terry Casey was head man at the Hughes yard for a few months. He had bought Hazy Dawn from Pat Hughes for Roly. Then Terry moved just down the road to the Mullins yard and Hazy Dawn went with him. Paddy Mullins recalls seeing the horse win a point-to-point at Gowran before it came to his yard and he reckoned that it was a very decent animal. He was very pleased with Terry Casey as head man. A native of Downings, Co. Donegal, Terry had a lot of experience in the racing business.

Terry served his time with the legendary Aubrey Brabazon on The Curragh and had worked with quite a few trainers around Ireland, north and south. After about three years he left the Mullins yard to set up on his own as a trainer in Wexford and later on at The Curragh, where he rented Brabazon's old stables, and Hazy Dawn went with him once more. He is now training in England, at Henfold House near Dorking, Surrey, and saddled Rough Quest, winner of the Ritz Club Chase at the Cheltenham Festival in 1995. Terry has fond memories of his years as head man to Paddy Mullins. 'I have a huge regard for Paddy,' he says. 'He is an absolute genius with horses. He pays huge attention to detail, and has all these little diaries as to when they were wormed, or when they had an injection. He is also very far-sighted. If a horse wins a race, he will have another race in mind for the horse perhaps a year ahead. He is a brilliant trainer, and a man of the highest integrity.'

While Terry worked at Doninga, he rented a cottage from Andrew MacMurrough Kavanagh, whose Borris House estate was just a few miles away from the yard. Terry himself rode in just a few races while with Paddy Mullins. On one occasion he fell while riding in a novice 'chase at Mallow and ended up in hospital with broken ribs and a punctured lung. Paddy came out into the yard next morning and found things in disarray. Recalls Terry with a grin, 'Paddy said in no uncertain terms to his wife Maureen that I would not be riding in races again – he needed me in the yard, not in hospital.'

He remembers that around the time he went to work for Paddy, Hazy Dawn had been injured in a point-to-point at Bray, Co. Wicklow. He recalls remarking to Paddy that his brother-in-law Roly Daniels had this mare and that she could make a fine 'chaser. Terry says, 'I remember Paddy immediately looking her up in the stud book and saying with obvious interest, "You could have a point there." The result was that Paddy put the mare in training for Cheltenham, with a great result in the end.'

There was a field of 26 runners as Hazy Dawn set out to run in the four mile National Hunt 'chase. Feature, ridden by Oliver Sherwood, was leading coming up to the 19th but made a mistake there and was headed by Yer Man, ridden by Anthony Powell. Willy Mullins had been waiting for the right moment to make his move and he now urged Hazy Dawn into contention, with Door Step, the mount of John Queally, also coming into the picture. Door Step made a mistake at the last and Hazy Dawn showed her staying power, moving well up the hill to win by seven lengths and three lengths from Door Step and Yer Man. It was St Patrick's Day, and thus all the more appropriate that the first, second and third places in the race should have gone to Irish horses.

Roly Daniels's wife Sarah, Terry's sister, could not make it to Cheltenham to see the mare run as she was ill. The race wasn't televised but she listened to the radio commentary at the couple's house in Co. Dublin and could not believe it when Hazy Dawn came first past the finish line. Says Sarah, 'We were hoping for a win, but we did not really expect it. I was absolutely thrilled when she won.'

Later that year, Hazy Dawn was to finish the season in magnificent style. She won the Burton Wood Amateur Hurdle at Punchestown on 10 November, with Willy again in the saddle. Ten days later, Hazy Dawn, ridden by T. V. Finn, won the Troytown Handicap Chase at Navan. Ultimately, Hazy Dawn developed tendon trouble, and went to stud. Roly and his wife have land attached to their home at Swords, and that's where Hazy Dawn has been since her retirement from racing. She has had five foals, including a couple of fillies, one by Orchestra and the other by Executive Perk. John Clarke, the lad who looked after Hazy Dawn at Doninga remembers well the horse – and the owner. 'Roly gave me a very generous present every Christmas,' he says.

During 1982, the Mullins stable was to notch up 41 winners – the same total as the previous year. Mrs Charmian Hill was still riding at this stage although the withdrawal of her jockey's licence was not far off. She rode her Diamond Do to success in the Brownstown Flat race at Navan on 21 April and then rode what was to be the best she ever owned when Dawn Run made her debut at Clonmel on 24 May, finishing unplaced. Mrs Hill went on to take fourth place with the mare in a race at Thurles on 17 June, and just six days later she rode Dawn Run to victory in the Castlemaine flat race at Tralee. This was to be Mrs Hill's last race ride, but at least she went out in style on the mare that was to become a legend. During 1982 another horse, Street Angel that was to prove a prolific winner for the stable made his debut at Listowel, winning the 'Goodwill' race. Street Angel went on to win seven more races for the stable in following seasons.

After his Cheltenham win on Hazy Dawn, Willy Mullins had another outing at Cheltenham the following year, but this time he felt fortunate to finish the course. He was riding Atha Cliath, which was owned by the late Des Hehir, who had a haulage business in Kilkenny. The horse had previously been owned by Ollie Freaney, renowned for his prowess at Gaelic football with the 1950s' Dublin team ('Atha Cliath' is Irish for Dublin), and one of Ireland's leading accountants. Ollie Freaney was an important owner at Doninga, having several horses at the yard. One of the better ones was Street Angel, who helped give Tony Mullins the Ritz Club trophy at Aintree in 1984. Tony won the trophy by gaining some crucial extra points when coming fourth in a race on Street Angel. Ollie Freaney had a stud farm in north Co. Dublin, and had owned racehorses for some time before he became a client at the Doninga yard. It happened that his sister, Mrs Frances Maguire was living in Bagenalstown and got to know Paddy and Maureen. Frances asked Ollie to send a horse to Doninga, and he went on to have several horses at the stable, including Atha Cliath.

Willy recalls, 'Atha Cliath was a funny horse. He would not jump a hurdle, he would gallop out through it, and had no regard for small fences. He would frighten the life out of you. But I always noticed that he jumped the regulations very well, far better than the others. We thought we'd bring him to Cheltenham and Aintree and have a crack at the two big hunter 'chases there. I thought the fences might suit him better. He went to the Foxhunter Chase at Cheltenham and jumped reasonably well. But about the ninth fence he never took off, galloped through it, trying one of his usual stunts. He did not fall, and I thought, Christ, this horse must be made of iron, to do that in the Foxhunters at Cheltenham and get away with it.

'We got around anyway and I said to the owner and to the

boss, let's bring this fellow to Aintree, and we won't school him from here until then, and he won't touch one of those fences in Aintree. And he went to Aintree about three weeks later and just gave me a dream of a ride. It was great to win. It was very brave of Des Hehir the owner, because the horse ran badly in Cheltenham, and it involved spending more money to go back and jump bigger fences. But Des was a very game owner and he said, "If you think he can do it, we'll have a crack at it." He jumped around the inside at Aintree as if he had been doing it all his life.'

Apart from the stars like Dawn Run and Atha Cliath, there were a lot of other horses winning races for the Doninga stable during 1983, giving the yard a total of 62 winners for the year. Dudie, ridden by Tony Mullins, won a maiden hurdle at Clonmel on 9 March that year, and went on to win a series of three other races before going on to 'chasing and recording a series of wins over fences. Dudie was to be entered for the Aintree Grand National, and Tony made the running for one clear round on him before falling early in the second circuit.

Another good horse for the stable at this period was Clanwilliam, owned by the late Charles Mansergh, of Greenane House, near Tipperary town. Mr Mansergh was a member of a prominent landowning family. He was a brother of the historian Dr Nicholas Mansergh and his nephew is Dr Martin Mansergh, Head of Research for the Fianna Fáil party. Willie Mullins won a bumper at Tramore in May on Clanwilliam, and his brother Tony was the rider when the horse won his maiden hurdle at Tipperary in October. Clanwilliam went on to win the valuable Guinness Handicap Hurdle at Clonmel in 1984 and, later that year, the Oranmore Dairies Handicap Hurdle at Galway. Meanwhile, as the stable moved in to the middle-1980s, the story of Doninga was to be dominated in a special way by one mare – Dawn Run . . .

CHAPTER 10

Jocked Off

Paddy Mullins will always remember the morning that Mrs Charmian Hill, owner of the most famous National Hunt horse he ever trained, the legendary Dawn Run, asked to have a word with him. The diminutive grandmother had just ridden out, as was her custom, at the stables in Doninga that morning. It was early in 1983 and Dawn Run had for some time been showing the promise that would take her to superstar status, that would put her up there among the greats like Arkle. Paddy's son Tony, the stable's number one jockey, had become the regular rider of the mare and of five races had won three and been placed once. Paddy sensed there was something wrong when Mrs Hill, who had been riding in races up to the previous year when her licence was withdrawn said, 'I must have a little chat with you.'

Paddy took her into the dining room. It's just off the hall and is the room where Paddy studies videos of races. There are valuable nineteenth-century racing prints on the walls, and arrayed on bookshelves is Paddy's big collection of form books. He knew they would not be disturbed in that room. Mrs Hill wasn't long in dropping her bombshell. She wanted Tony 'jocked off' Dawn Run. She didn't want him riding when the mare made her debut at the Cheltenham Festival that year. Paddy was stunned.

Says Paddy, 'I'd be the first to change jockeys if I could see the reason for it, but I cannot ever remember any time I could blame Tony for anything as regards the way he rode Dawn Run and the mare certainly performed for him like she never performed for anyone else. That was the thing that niggled me and Maureen. If I thought that changing jockeys was better for the horse I would not have objected. I would certainly have put down Tony and I could have put him down more easily than putting down anyone else. But her mind was made up. She didn't want Tony riding the mare in Cheltenham. It was a bit of a shock to me. She said to me, "Can you get another jockey?" and I said that I could. I didn't debate the matter with her. It was her prerogative.'

Maureen sensed there was a problem when she saw Mrs Hill going off for a private chat with her husband. Maureen was on tenterhooks waiting to ask Paddy what the problem was – and she too was shocked by the news that her son was being rejected as Dawn Run's 'partner' at Cheltenham that March. Paddy reckons it was Maureen who broke the news to Tony. Dawn Run, who was to become the greatest mare in the recent history of National Hunt racing, had cast the first of many shadows over the Mullins household, the final shadow being when the gallant mare herself was killed in France.

After Mrs Hill's rejection of his son, the Doninga trainer thought long and hard about an alternative jockey and came up with an English-based rider, the veteran Irish-born Ron Barry. Mrs Hill approved the choice. Barry rode Dawn Run into second place to Sabin Du Loir at the Sun Alliance Hurdle at the Cheltenham Festival on 16 March. Tony then partnered the mare over her next four hurdle races, with three wins and one second place. But despite this fine record, Cheltenham 1984 was looming up again, and Mrs Hill asked for another dreaded 'little chat' with Paddy in the dining room at Doninga. He could predict what was coming. Mrs Hill didn't want Tony to ride the mare at the next Cheltenham Festival either, when Dawn Run's target would be the Champion Hurdle. Recalls Paddy, 'I decided to get Jonjo O'Neill. Everyone thought it was Mrs Hill who picked Jonjo, but it was not. It was I who selected him. She approved my choice. I was shocked on both occasions at her request for another jockey because Tony had done nothing wrong on the mare, and the mare had always run her heart out for Tony.'

He believes that Mrs Hill remained extremely resentful that she herself was not allowed by the authorities to ride Dawn Run in races. And he believes her feelings of resentment against the authorities were not assuaged by the fact that it was a very young jockey, Tony Mullins, aged only about 20, who was getting the rides that she felt she should have been getting.

Paddy Mullins is at pains to point out that he had then, and still has, the height of respect and regard for Mrs Hill. While they had their differences, they never had an argument or a confrontation. So far as he was concerned, she always carried out her responsibilities as an owner to the letter. Says Paddy, 'There was never an open difference between me and Mrs Hill over Tony. Our relationship stayed the same all the way through. There was never a question of a break – on either side. She was a very good owner. Her responsibilities were adhered to – not just in terms of payment but in every way. Of course I would have wished Tony to get the chance to ride the mare in the big races at Cheltenham. She knew how I felt but she also knew she was in the driving seat, and sentiment, I think, never entered her mind.

'She never gave a hint that she was in any way critical of anything I did with the horses – except where Tony was concerned. She only took a dislike to Tony's connection with the horse because he was getting into the saddle that she thought was hers. My firm belief is that this was all she ever had against Tony. He was usurping her seat in the saddle. When she rejected Tony she said she wanted a more experienced rider. It was my opinion that the mare would run better for the "inexperienced youngster". But I had to respect her views. I did not argue with her or give a counter viewpoint. She earned my respect because she never specified an alternative rider. She left the entire booking of the rider to me – Ron Barry and later Jonjo O'Neill.'

Unfortunately for Tony Mullins, while he got on well with the mare, he feels he didn't get on well with the owner. In his view, there was never a rapport between himself and Mrs Hill. He says, 'Mrs Hill used to come to the yard to ride out. She would ride out every Monday, and sometimes on a Wednesday as well. The one thing I remember is that she would say hello to everyone in the yard, but she would never say hello to me. And this was before Dawn Run ever appeared.' Tony himself can't recall very much about the first time he rode Dawn Run in a race, except that she powered up to the line in a maiden hurdle at Navan in December 1982 and won easily. He thought the mare showed promise but did not fully realise what he was dealing with until the second time he rode her, just a few days later. It was in the Findus Beefburger Hurdle during the Christmas meeting in Leopardstown. And it was on this occasion that he came to realise, with mounting excitement, that this was the kind of animal that you might only have the good fortune to encounter once in a lifetime.

Tony recalls, 'My brother Willy was riding a horse called Castletown House and they thought he was a machine, he could go so fast. And I knew in the ring the way my father was talking that he thought Willy's horse would win. And I jumped out in front on Dawn Run and she started powering down the track and I can still remember it. This was a novice horse, but she went down to the first and let fly, and I said to myself, "This one is special." And every time since, she was always a step ahead of you. Other horses would do it when they would be asked, but she knew what she was at. She was unbelievable to ride. You could almost feel her thinking.

'When you'd go to the third or fourth last and you would be starting to step up a gear, before you would go to change your hands she would quicken for you. She would know when she was going to be asked to quicken and go. The way she used to attack fences when horses were trying to challenge her was incredible. She would just give you a feeling that I never got off any horse – even the best of horses. None of them was ever like Dawn Run. None of them. She showed it from almost the beginning.' Another person who noticed the power of Dawn Run from an early stage was the lad who looked after her, John

Clarke. The youth from Bagenalstown rode out Dawn Run probably more than anybody else in the mare's lifetime – even Mrs Hill. At the Findus event in Leopardstown, John decided to take a chance with the mare and he had a tenner on the nose at 12–1. The mare didn't let him down and he was most grateful to her for the nice 'touch' that was landed that day.

The Mullins family was to encounter joy and sorrow in equal measure with Dawn Run, who was to become Ireland's best-loved racehorse since Arkle, a major sports 'personality' in her own right, with a series of wins that have ensured the Mullins yard a special place in the history books. The mare brought enormous prestige to the stable but the fact that Tony was 'jocked off' at the insistence of the owner, is still a sore point – so much so that it is not discussed in the family circle to this day. Tony Mullins still feels that Mrs Hill was unfair to him. Mrs Hill, the wife of a doctor who lived about a 45 minute drive from the Mullins yard, was a lot more than just the traditional passive owner. Apart from riding out on a regular basis at Doninga, she was a skilled amateur jockey in her own right, and rode many winners. She was overjoyed when she rode Dawn Run to victory in a bumper at Tralee in June 1982. For the mare, it was to be the first of many wins and, ironically for the jockey, it was to mark the close of her race riding career. The Turf Club decided that Mrs Hill was too old to continue riding in races, and she was devastated to lose her licence as a jockey. Dawn Run thus gave the galloping granny her last win and her last race ride. She was appalled at the thought that she could no longer partner her beloved mare in races.

Despite the fact that she was aged 62, Mrs Hill wanted to continue riding for the foreseeable future, and Paddy and Maureen are convinced that she wanted to partner Dawn Run all the way to the Gold Cup at Cheltenham. Says Paddy, 'She just wanted to keep going. She would have ridden in the Aintree Grand National if they had let her. She knew no fear. It was as if the part of the brain that produces nerves and anxiety had been removed from her at birth.' After a race in Clonmel, during which Mrs Hill was unshipped by her horse, Paddy recalls being challenged by a steward. He was told in no uncertain terms that this woman would have to be stopped from riding. Mrs Hill's husband Eddie happened to be present and Paddy introduced him to the steward, who made the same point vigorously to Dr Hill, that she would have to be stopped. Dr Hill, knowing more than anyone about his wife's determination, replied, 'You stop her!' After Mrs Hill lost her licence, she had to content herself with riding out on Dawn Run at Doninga. Tony Mullins became Dawn Run's regular jockey, after his younger brother Tom notched up a couple of wins on the mare.

Riding Dawn Run was always, for Tony, an enormously exciting experience that was guaranteed to get the adrenaline racing. He firmly believes that some riders get on with particular horses, and he considers that he had an extremely good 'working relationship' with Dawn Run. In partnership with the mare he began to accumulate the wins. He was in the saddle when she won the Page Three Handicap Hurdle at Liverpool in April 1983, his fourth win on the mare. Head travelling lad Jim Murphy recalls how, after that win, he was handed an envelope full of cash by Page Three model Linda Lusardi. 'I was as red as beetroot,' recalls Jim. 'I got a fierce slagging afterwards from the lads back in the yard.'

The following day, at the same venue, Dawn Run obliged again by winning the Sun Templegate Hurdle. By then, Mrs Hill was making long-term plans for Cheltenham 1984, and Tony did not figure in those plans, and after her 'little chat' with Paddy, Jonjo O'Neill had been called in. Jonjo recalls his surprise at getting a phone call out of the blue from Paddy Mullins asking him if he would ride the mare. Jonjo doesn't believe he ever had any contact with Paddy before that. And he didn't have to think twice about taking the ride that was being offered to him – it was the chance of a lifetime. He became aware of the tension over Tony being jocked off, but at the same time, he says that everybody involved was very professional. 'We just got on with it,' Jonjo says. 'It's hard for any rider to be jocked off. As a trainer myself I have not had to do it. It's always very awkward when it happens. But I always remained on very good terms with Tony. There was never any rift between myself and Tony – or Paddy.'

Jonjo began partnering the mare in November 1983, and rode her to a win that month in the VAT Watkins Hurdle at Ascot. Jonjo knew that the mare was being aimed at the Champion Hurdle, and began to wonder if she was really up to it. Dawn Run had won at Ascot by just a short head from Amarach and Jonjo expressed his reservations to Paddy Mullins. But the trainer knew of what the mare was capable. Jonjo and Dawn Run went on to land the Christmas Hurdle at Kempton, by a head, and the Wessel Champion Hurdle at Leopardstown. Then the duo carried off one of the biggest victories in the mare's career, the Champion Hurdle at Cheltenham. Jonjo's ride to victory, on 13 March 1984, sparked off incredible scenes of jubilation among the big Irish crowd.

Jonjo was injured later that month, the day before he was due to ride Dawn Run in the Sandeman Aintree Hurdle at Liverpool on 31 March. Jonjo was bitterly disappointed. Says Paddy Mullins, 'There was some debate as to whether Jonjo could ride or not and finally the doctors said to him, "No you can't ride." I went to Mrs Hill and said to her, "Can Tony ride?" And she said, "I'm not that bad, of course he can." Tony and the mare had a ten-length win in the Sandeman over Very Promising. And then Tony was on her for the French Champion Hurdle. And he did so well on her, going on to win the first 'chase on the mare, at Navan, I thought that Tony was here to stay, but how wrong I was.' During his 'comeback' period with Dawn Run, Tony won a remarkable six races in succession, including the French Champion Hurdle in June 1984, and embarked with the mare on her 'chasing career. It became almost routine for Tony and the mare not only to win but to win by many lengths. But when it came to the really big event, the Gold Cup of 1986, Tony would once again lose the ride on the mare. For the Mullins family, there was as much agony as ecstasy in the saga of Dawn Run . . .

CHAPTER 11

Dawn Run Makes History

Tony Mullins gave up riding in 1992 because of back injury problems and he is training at Gowran, Co. Kilkenny, just a few miles from the old family stables at Doninga. He lives with his jockey wife Mags and their two children in a house just outside the village of Gowran. Tony is philosophical about the Dawn Run saga but it is clear he has his regrets. His big regret is that he never rode a winner at the Cheltenham Festival. It is clear that he feels he could have won with Dawn Run in both the Champion Hurdle and the Gold Cup. But while he has regrets, he says he doesn't have resentment. The big prize of Cheltenham Festival glory has eluded him but he has other great memories to look back on, especially as regards Dawn Run.

Relaxing in his sitting room, with various trophies from his racing career on the sideboard, he recalls the good times and the bad times with Dawn Run, and the impact the mare had on the Mullins family. He says, 'The Dawn Run saga was difficult because, first of all, I was first jockey in the yard and I had really not done anything wrong on the mare to lead to me being jocked off. A lot of people probably thought that I was only riding her because I was the son of the trainer Paddy Mullins and not because I was first jockey at Doninga. It was all very difficult. You have enough pressure coming up to a big race without these added pressures. There was a lot of pressure on my father. I just thought, and I still believe, that Mrs Hill was unfair to jock me down. And having jocked me down I got back up and I was jocked down again.

'Owners have the right to say who they want to ride a horse, but Mrs Hill had never before done anything like this. Maybe she was being advised by others. When you have a good horse the number of people telling you what to do or where to go is incredible. I remember asking my father at home one night, "What do you think is the most difficult part of racing?" And he said that to be the owner of a good horse is the most difficult part of racing because you are trying to be advised by your trainer and you are definitely being advised by about 50 people on the way home from the races.'

Tony began riding in races in 1976 while he was still at school. The following year, in a point-to-point at Gowran, he was riding a horse called Creidim, owned by his mother's brother George Doran, when disaster struck. The horse fell at the second last, suffered a broken neck and was killed, while Tony sustained a broken leg. He was on crutches for almost a year and missed so much school – he was just coming up to the Leaving Certificate – that he decided to leave school and go to Peter Cundell's yard in England. His father knew Cundell through selling horses to him. In 1979 he was back in Doninga for a summer break. His brother Willy was found to be too heavy to ride a horse called Pearlstone in Tramore. Tony rode instead and won. He had fully intended to go back to England but he started riding winners and decided to stay on. In January 1980 he turned professional, deciding that he should try to make some money out of his riding. Because he had had ten winners as an amateur he was not allowed to become an apprentice to his father. He had to carry the penalties with him and become a fully-fledged jockey. He did well as a professional. He was the champion claiming rider in 1982; joint champion with Frank Berry in 1984, with 50 winners each, and champion jockey for the year 1988–89. He is particularly proud of his latter achievement because he only rode hurdle races that year. He had developed back trouble – a common complaint among jump jockeys – and decided that he would not be much good at riding over fences because of the problems with his back. Eventually his back troubles became so bad that he had to give up riding in races altogether. He still suffers excruciating back pain from time to time.

Tony has a lot of stories and a lot of memories to do with Dawn Run. While, like his father, he loves horses but is generally not sentimental about them, the exception is Dawn Run, or 'the mare' as she was always affectionately known. He talks of her fondly as if she were a valued, brilliant but sometimes irascible old friend who has come to a tragic end. Tony, like his father, believes that somewhere along the line, Dawn Run's genes became mixed up, and that she should really have been a male. She had a lot of macho male aggressive traits. On one occasion, while veterinary surgeon Paddy Fennelly was trying to give her an injection, the mare sent him flying with a well-aimed kick to the chest from one of her front hooves. A horrified Maureen Mullins thought the vet, who has been attending the Mullins horses for 25 years and is a valued family friend, had been killed. But he landed in straw and luckily was uninjured.

Tony says, 'Dawn Run was not the quiet lady that some people believe. She was a savage. She was a demon to get a cover on or off. You would literally have to have a lad holding her while you were doing it, unless you knew her really well. She wasn't the lovely little Irish mare that some people think she was – she was a big masculine type of mare. When you are at horses all your life, without looking underneath you would know the difference between a filly and a colt, but you would not know with her – she had all the features of a gelding. From the back, she had that big square backside with the second leg as they call it, the extra muscle coming down that only colts or geldings have. I would imagine she was half masculine.'

Tony has always been on good terms with the ever-cheerful, outgoing Jonjo and they meet from time to time. Says Tony, 'I get on great with Jonjo. We are very friendly. We often meet for meals even still. I had a meal with him recently in the Berkeley Court Hotel in Dublin. I did not feel any resentment to anybody involved in the Dawn Run affair, and I certainly never felt any resentment towards Jonjo.' Still, as Tony watched Jonjo steer Dawn Run to the mare's first win at the Cheltenham Festival to take the glittering prize of the Champion Hurdle, he could be forgiven for wishing that it was he, not Jonjo, who was in the saddle. The connections were always confident about the outcome. The night before the race, Mrs Hill and her husband Eddie held an impromptu champagne party for about 20 guests at the Cotswold Grange Hotel. The next morning Mrs Hill did not follow her occasional early morning custom of riding out Dawn Run. She told a reporter, 'I have left everything in the hands of my trainer, and I couldn't ask for better in Paddy Mullins.'

As the race itself got under way, Dawn Run, the 5/4 on favourite, took the initiative, with another racing legend, Desert Orchid, joining her at the third flight and leading for a short way. But Dawn Run was back in the lead at the fifth, and was not headed again. Another Irish hope, Buck House, partnered by Tommy Carmody, challenged down the hill but made a mistake two flights from home. Cima, a 66–1 outsider whose prospects few had rated highly, then moved into second place. Dawn Run came over the last hurdle about one and a half lengths in front, with Cima, ridden by Peter Scudamore, continuing to gain ground. Dawn Run edged to her right in the closing stages but caused no serious interference and took the coveted prize by three-quarters of a length. Very Promising made late progress to take third place and Buck House was fourth. Dawn Run was the first odds-on Champion Hurdle winner since Bula in 1972, and the first mare to win the race since African Sister in 1939.

A large part of the ecstatic Irish crowd invaded the unsaddling enclosure and several burly sets of shoulders hoisted Mrs Hill aloft. Jonjo became frightened as he was surrounded by the crowd, for a couple of idiotic punters tried to grab pieces of his tack as souvenirs, presumably not realising that if Jonjo could not weigh in with all his equipment, the unthinkable would happen and Dawn Run would be disqualified. Jonjo finally managed to fight his way into the comparative calm of the weigh-room. Some observers said they had not seen such scenes of jubilation since Arkle defeated Mill House in the Gold Cup 20 years before. It was suggested to Cima's trainer, Jim Old, that he might have grounds for an objection but, overawed by Dawn Run's reception, he sportingly declared, 'How can I object in the face of that?' Tony Power, writing in the *Irish Press*, reported how the trainer's wife 'wept unashamedly' while Paddy, always a shy man, 'quietly slipped away into the weigh-room'.

Ironically, the huge wave of cheering that rose up from the Irish as Dawn Run powered home came close to stopping the mare from winning the race – at least in the opinion of the man in the saddle that day, Jonjo O'Neill. According to Jonjo, the crescendo of cheering caused the mare to lapse at the last hurdle. For one terrible moment he was afraid she might stop running because of being 'spooked' by the 'Irish roar'. But the mare was made of sterner stuff, and continued on course.

The day after Dawn Run had done Doninga proud, there was another moment of Cheltenham glory for the stable, when another of Paddy Mullins's charges, Macks Friendly, partnered by his son Willy, won the National Hunt Chase. The horse had been sold by Willy to flamboyant Dublin businessman and racing personality John Mulhern just hours before the race. An emissary from the Mullins family had contacted Mulhern earlier in the week to see if he was interested in buying the horse that would probably win the National Hunt four mile 'chase. Mulhern said it would be bad luck to buy a horse on the 13th, but he would be prepared to do business the following day, if somebody would be good enough to phone him at his hotel, and so the deal was clinched, less than 24 hours before the race itself.

Willy recalls a moment of near panic during the 'chase, when, out in front, he feared that he had strayed onto the wrong course. With a slightly sore head from the Champion Hurdle victory celebrations the night before, he remembers coming up to the fifth last, going well, and thinking that if he got over this safely then he was in with a chance. 'I thought to myself, "All I have to do is keep my head and keep jumping . . . "' He kept going well, there was nothing in front of him, and finally he came around the last bend. He looked out for the final fence –

but it wasn't there, or at least he couldn't see it. 'You can imagine how I felt. I had everything done, all I had to do was jump the last fence, and it was not there. For one terrible moment I thought I had strayed onto the hurdle track.' Then, suddenly, to his great relief, he saw the fence.

What had happened was that the shadow of the stand falling over the dark fence had created an optical illusion, making the fence 'disappear' just for a moment. Says Willy, 'I went down to the fence, jumped it, and could hear something coming behind me. I just put down the head and kept going and the winning post came up. In fact we won quite well. I don't think there was any danger.' Coming in six lengths behind to take second place was the Michael Morris-trained Red Shah, ridden by A. J. Martin while Mister Donut was third. There had been a big gamble on Macks Friendly and he started at 11–4. John Mulhern declined to say afterwards how much he had paid for the horse. He declared, 'The money is irrelevant, it's the sport that counts!'

The year 1984 was an incredible year for Paddy Mullins. Apart from Dawn Run's achievements and the Macks Friendly win at Cheltenham, there were many other successes. Paddy was operating at full blast on so many fronts. The season was to prove the pinnacle of his career to date, with a massive tally of 109 winners for the year. During that year, Tony Mullins won the Ritz Club trophy for leading jockey at Aintree, and the stable also had its moments of glory on the Flat. On the same day, 31 March, that Dawn Run won the Sandeman Hurdle at Liverpool, another Mullins charge, Girl In Blue, ridden by Stephen Craine, was taking the Irish Lincolnshire back home at The Curragh. It was the first time Paddy Mullins won the Lincolnshire and the fact that Girl In Blue was bred and owned by his wife made the victory all the sweeter for the Doninga stable.

Also in 1984, another Mullins-trained horse, Chammsky, won the Irish Cambridgeshire. When Chammsky first came to the Mullins yard he was seen as a difficult horse to handle until, as often happens, somebody discovered the 'key' to getting the best from him. In this particular case it was Tom Mullins who found the 'key' – he discovered that Chammsky ran best when his rider did not carry a whip. For the rest of his career at the Mullins stable, jockeys rode Chammsky without laying a stick on him. In November 1984, Chammsky, owned by Mrs Mercy Jennings of Ballinrobe, Co. Mayo, was taken to America to run in the Colonial Cup at Camden, South Carolina, with Tony Mullins as the jockey. Chammsky ran a disappointing race, but still impressed a leading American trainer Burley Cox, who bought him for the racehorse owner, Richard Dupont III.

It was also the year when a young man who was later to become Irish National Hunt champion jockey, Charlie Swan, began riding for Paddy Mullins. Paddy offered the youngster a ride on Ash Creek at Tramore in June. Charlie had no transport, so his mother drove him to the racecourse from The Curragh. Charlie had his first winner that day, riding Ash Creek to victory in the Waterford Crystal Handicap Trophy. The partners went on to take two valuable handicaps that year, the Hennessy at Leopardstown in July and the McDonagh at the Galway Festival later that month. Ararun and Hungary Hur both won bumpers that year, and went on to win quite a few races for the stable.

* * *

Tony Mullins and his father had their ups and downs with Dawn Run, and certainly one of the better moments had to be when Tony rode the mare to victory in the French Champion Hurdle at Auteuil. The race took place in June 1984, just a few months after the Champion Hurdle victory. For some time, Paddy had had his sights on the Auteuil event as a suitable target for Dawn Run. Having won the Irish and English Champion Hurdles, it seemed like a logical move to go for the equivalent event in France.

Paddy had, of course, known the Auteuil course since attending races there while on honeymoon back in 1954. He had sent Herring Gull there to win the Prix des Drags in 1970, and his knowledge of the course and, indeed, of French racing was given the final finishing touches towards the end of the 1970s when he and a number of other trainers were brought out from Ireland to France as guests of the French jump racing authorities. With the experience gained from this and other trips to France, Paddy was undoubtedly one of the best-informed and most experienced of the Irish trainers as regards French jump racing coming into the 1980s. And his investment of time and trouble in learning the intricacies of French racing was to pay off handsomely in the case of Dawn Run.

Paddy decided that the mare would go to France for a week's schooling and to run in the 'prep' race for the Champion Hurdle, the Prix La Barka, in May 1984. After the Prix La Barka, the mare would then tackle the big event itself about three weeks later. Tony recalls with humour the funnier side of that first trip to France with Dawn Run. 'My father was very much on edge because he had sort of pushed for me to ride the horse. He was afraid first of all that he might not be going with the right horse. It was a dicey thing to do, unknown territory. Jonjo had broken his leg and was out. My father was anxious. We had not discussed it but I knew it. We arrived in France and got on this little metro, a real old one, and we arrived in Maisons-Laffitte. Once my mother got going, she was flying. She loves going to France. We got off the train and our bones were shaking. I had my riding gear, my own gear and my mother's gear, and I was trying to carry the three up the steps of the metro. Then my father says "Where's the hotel?" "Oh," she says, "don't worry about that – we'll get that in a minute." He says again, "Where's the hotel?" Then she says, "I never booked one."

'Well he started to get in a state and he had himself very worried. Then she sees a boutique, says, "Look at this" and she flies across the road to look at it. She is over at the window and I am coming behind with the cases. He says, "How are we going to get a hotel? We're going to have to sleep in the park." With that, the mother who is looking at the prices of the things in the boutique says, "Don't worry about that – we'll get a taxi now." Maisons-Laffitte is some way out of Paris and my father turns to her and says, "A taxi in Maisons-Laffitte – you might as well be looking for an aeroplane in Goresbridge!" I will never forget it. He doesn't like being away from home – the tension of the race, and being away from the yard, affects him. It was so funny looking back on it now. As it happens, they did get a taxi – and a hotel.'

Tony also recalls with amusement Paddy's reaction to the French custom of shaking hands with everyone in sight. 'We had the mare in a livery yard outside Paris and when you came in every morning there might be as many as a dozen people around the yard and you would have to shake hands with them all. After three or four mornings of this, getting closer to the race, you could see from the boss's face he was getting annoyed with this. He came in one morning anyway and would not shake hands. He says to me, "I'm doing no more of that shaking hands – that's only spreading germs." That was his excuse.'

Dawn Run won the Prix La Barka easily. In Paddy's words, 'She cantered in.' The mare had easily beaten a number of class horses, with World Citizen second, Network third and Seidhr fourth. The next day the French racing newspaper *Paris-Turf* was ecstatic about Dawn Run. The hard-bitten and hard-to-impress journalists of the Paris racing bible were reaching for the superlatives to describe the performance of the Irish mare. Over a headline in rather awkward English, 'Very well, Dawn Run' the newspaper also published a picture of Paddy, in trench coat and cap, chatting with Tony and Mrs Hill. The caption remarked how they were all smiling even before the race – a sign of their confidence, the newspaper concluded.

After her runaway victory in the Prix La Barka, the mare came home for a while, returning for the big event at Auteuil on 22 June. Maureen Mullins has a most evocative picture taken on the morning of the big race, showing a very youthful Tony and his brother Tom, with the mare, in the lush greenery of the racecourse at Maisons-Laffitte, where she was being schooled. Also in the picture is the travelling head lad who usually accompanied Dawn Run, Jim Murphy. All three are still in their twenties, and this youthful team from a quiet townland in Co.

Kilkenny would, later that day, be taking on some of the most sophisticated stables in Europe.

The evening before, a French photographer went with Tony to the final hurdle at the Auteuil track where the big race would be entering its closing stages. He wanted to get a picture of Dawn Run coming over the final obstacle, with the Eiffel Tower in the background, and he needed to find out where he should be positioned to get such a picture. Tony showed him where Dawn Run would be crossing this final hurdle and, with all the confidence of youth, explained that the mare would be out in front by herself at this stage, with the rest of the field trailing quite some distance behind. Everything worked out as Tony had predicted, and the photographer got his unique photograph. Jim Murphy has a copy of the picture, and it's one of his most prized possessions – so much so that he asked an artist to do a painting based on the photo. To this day, the painting hangs proudly on a wall of his sitting room at his home near Goresbridge, where he runs a stud farm.

On the morning of the big race, the Doninga team, after breakfast at the Café Bleu, were full of confidence as they put Dawn Run through her paces at the schooling grounds at Maisons-Laffitte. The mare was in the form of her life that day. Tony, smoking a cigarette when he got the chance, took her over some hurdles and called out in delight, 'Oh boy, didn't she leap!' The soft-spoken man always referred to in the stable as 'the boss' made his usual quiet entry onto the scene. Paddy Mullins could see that the mare was in excellent shape and that she would slaughter the opposition. But he was rarely a man for superlatives, and when journalist Brough Scott approached him as Tony and Tom hosed down the mare, he made one of his usual, laconic, low-key comments. 'I think she is in fine form,' he said in his quiet way. Looking back on it now, he would go a little stronger than that. 'The mare was like a LION that day,' he says. 'She was extraordinary.'

It was a drive of about a dozen kilometres from the schooling ground to the Bois de Boulogne and to the racecourse there, Auteuil, the premier jump track in France. Members of the

144

Irish contingent were, understandably, all keyed up as the race got under way. Paddy's son Tom was there, and he recalls that there were not many people on the stand where they watched the race. In the early stages of the event, one of Tom's friends called out 'Come on, Dawn Run.' Instinctively, Tom shouted the same words, which rang out awkwardly in the comparative silence. Paddy, who was standing in front of Tom, was not impressed. Tom recalls with a grin, 'He turned around, and shut me up with a glance. I didn't say another word.' As it turned out, the Irish on the stand need not have worried about the mare. There was really no contest. By the time she was around the first bend, she was out on her own. Irish shouts of 'ya boy ya' mingled with the slightly more elegant French cries of 'bravo'.

Of all Dawn Run's marvellous wins, Paddy was to find the victory in this event the most personally satisfying because of the challenges the mare was able to face down during the contest. The fact that it was his own son in the saddle no doubt added to the pleasure. Paddy recalls, 'Daniel Wildenstein, the wealthy antiques dealer and a big owner in France, had two horses in the race and was absolutely moving heaven and earth to win it. I think he had very little regard for Dawn Run before the race, although he must have had some, for they had worked out tactics to beat the mare. The tactics were that one of these Wildenstein horses was to jump out, to pace Dawn Run and bring the mare off her legs, and the other fellow would come then and win.

'Neither of them got within many lengths of Dawn Run and she came home alone – they were never able to get to her. Dawn Run showed them a clean pair of heels and won easily. The better fancied of the two Wildenstein horses went on to win one of the group races at Longchamp on the Flat that year, the French St Leger. Dawn Run was really taking on something there.' As the race started, Tony sent the mare straight into the lead. The mare held a six-length lead over Video Tape and World Citizen going out onto the back straight for the first time, and throughout the race none of her nine rivals got closer to her than six lengths. Mister Jack proved to be the best of her pursuers, coming in second, six lengths behind the mare, with Salute in third place.

Dawn Run became the only racehorse ever to win the Irish, English and French Champion Hurdles, and Paddy Mullins became the only trainer from Ireland or the UK to have a win in the French event. Paddy's investment of time and trouble in learning the intricacies and the peculiarities of French racing had paid incredible dividends. It was all a far cry from the time he first visited Auteuil during his honeymoon a full 30 years earlier, when he was present simply as a humble spectator.

There was jubilation among the small Irish contingent after the race. Mrs Hill was ecstatic and any suggestion of a lack of rapport between herself and Tony was forgotten in the euphoria of the moment. Tony, always a well-mannered young man, was deferential to the elderly owner. 'I had a lot left in the tank, Ma'am,' he remarked to her with understandable pride. Daniel Wildenstein approached Paddy and Maureen. He offered his congratulations and paid the mare a rare compliment. 'Dawn Run is the best I have ever seen over hurdles,' said the man who was one of the leading racehorse owners in Europe at the time. If Wildenstein had previously harboured any doubts about the ability of Dawn Run, they were dispelled by the mare's performance that day.

Meanwhile the celebrations began among the dozen or so friends of the younger members of the Mullins family from the Carlow-Kilkenny region who usually travelled to 'support' Dawn Run like football fans would travel to support their favourite football team. Tony remembers the laughs he had with one old pal from Graiguenamanagh, Ollie Haire. Ollie used to work as a lad at the Doninga stables and would ride out. Later, he had become an enthusiastic punter and was called the Ginger Kid. (The title was conferred on Ollie when he was struggling through a crowd to place a bet with the bookmaker Sean Graham Snr. The bookie spotted a valued client in the crush and called out, 'Make way, make way, for the Ginger Kid.' The nickname stuck.)

After Dawn Run had demolished the opposition at Auteuil,

a journalist approached Ollie and asked him why, as a fervent follower of the mare, he had no binoculars to watch her in action. Ollie, who made a killing by betting heavily on Dawn Run that day, and whose pockets were bulging with French francs, answered, 'Sure why would I need binoculars – didn't I know that Dawn Run would be out in front the whole way!' (Ollie was to die suddenly at a tragically early age in August 1994. He was home on a trip from Australia at the time, and a couple of days previously, for old time's sake, had ridden out at Doninga. Tony was stunned by his death.)

At a reception after the race, Mrs Hill made a prediction that was to come true with a vengeance. She gave a quote to a correspondent for the *Sporting Life*, who published her comment in the next edition of that newspaper, and the quote was this, 'Dawn Run will win the Gold Cup in two years time.' Tony Mullins didn't have time to hang around to join in the festivities. He changed out of his riding gear, somebody brought him champagne, and he drank it while waiting for a taxi to arrive to take him to the plane. When he reached the airport, he realised he didn't have his passport. To keep it safe, he had left it with Dawn Run's passport, and in all the excitement had forgotten to retrieve it. But he was let through and onto the plane for Dublin. He recalls, 'I won the race at 3.30 p.m., and I was sitting down having a drink in a lad's house in Carlow at 9.30 p.m. That's how quick it was. My passport came home with the mare.'

After the French Champion Hurdle, Dawn Run spent the summer at her owner's secluded place near Waterford. Mrs Hill lived in a rambling period residence with parkland stretching down to the shores of the River Suir estuary. Paddy Mullins used to attend a 'pool party' there every year before the races at Tramore. He always enjoyed the party. Food would be laid out around the swimming pool and guests could have a swim if they wanted to. Mrs Hill herself always had a swim during the party. Says Paddy, 'Mrs Hill had a lovely piece of land there. The tide used to come in on the land and I always felt that this must have helped an awful lot towards the minerals the horses were ingesting. All the horses reared there were fairly decent.'

There was an extraordinary episode during Dawn Run's summer break with her owner. Somebody left a gate open and Dawn Run, one of the most valuable animals in Ireland or Britain at the time, and two other horses, went missing. Mrs Hill found them wandering in a housing estate two miles away. But she was kicked in the thigh when she tried to round them up and the three ran off. The animals were found safe and sound next morning in a local field, Dawn Run clearly having enjoyed her night away from home. If there was a ringleader among the horses who made their getaway it was undoubtedly Dawn Run. Paddy Mullins's daughter Sandra has a vivid memory of looking across a hedge into a field at Doninga and seeing the mare's proud head held high as she led the other horses in an impromptu canter. 'There was no doubt as to who was the boss in the pecking order among the horses,' says Sandra.

After her summer break, the mare returned to Doninga to be prepared for 'chasing, and in November that year, Tony opened the mare's campaign over fences with a run in the Nobber Chase at Navan. But while he had a win, the mare suffered an injury and was out for a year. One of the more notable achievements during 1985 for the Mullins stable was the victory of Bermuda Classic in the valuable Railway Stakes at The Curragh on 29 June with Brent Thompson riding. She followed this with another win at The Curragh the following month, this time taking the Nishapour Stakes in the hands of Willie Carson. Bermuda Classic was owned by Pat O'Riordan who originally came from the Goresbridge area. Pat worked in the tourism industry in Bermuda and once turned up at the Phoenix Park in yellow Bermuda shorts to see his mare run. It has to be said that Pat was always magnanimous in victory. On one occasion, when Bermuda Classic beat one of Sheikh Mohamed's horses by a short head, he tried to console the Arab billionaire by patting him on the shoulder and remarking, 'Sorry about that, boss.' Tony Mullins recalls how it was his father's passionate interest in pedigrees that first led to the acquisition of Bermuda Classic.

'He bought her as a two-year-old because her ninth dam was Pretty Polly, one of the greatest fillies that ever raced,' says Tony. Among other horses to serve the stable well during 1985, which saw a total number of 94 winners recorded for the yard, were Brideswell Dew and Proud Souroma. Each horse scored several wins.

In December 1985 Dawn Run was back in action with a vengeance. Tony rode the mare to victory in the Durkan Brothers Chase at Punchestown, and this was followed by a win in the Sean P. Graham Chase during the Christmas meeting at Leopardstown, when the mare saw off a challenge from another great National Hunt star, Buck House.

The scene was set for an attempt on the really big prize – the Cheltenham Gold Cup. The mare's 'sighter' for the Gold Cup was the Holsten Distributors Chase at the January 1986 Cheltenham meeting. Dawn Run dominated the race from the start and had the field strung out behind her as she approached the last open ditch. The mare misjudged the fence and hit it hard, and Tony was unseated. He was thrown around the mare's neck on the off side, but, incredibly, managed to land on his feet and retain hold of the reins. Some observers reckon that if he had landed on the near side he would have been in a much better position to re-mount the mare and continue.

He proceeded to get back into the saddle anyway as the rest of the field swept by. Many years on, he says, 'When I got back up on the mare I thought to myself for a second I could catch up. I could have pulled up, and then I said to myself, "Why let the mare leave Cheltenham with a sour taste, when she is coming back here in six weeks time for the Gold Cup?" I said I'd let her pop down over the four fences, which I did, and I'd say that it was a big help to her. You will get horses that got a hard race as a young horse on a particular race track, and they will never produce it again on that track.'

He will never forget the scene back in the parade ring. Mrs Hill, who had expected another Dawn Run victory, was devastated that her beloved mare trailed in fourth and last. Recalls Tony, 'She believed her mare was almighty and unbeatable. It was just her sincere belief and she wasn't trying to be awkward. I will never forget the shock and horror in her face when I came in that day. The thought of her mare not winning! She just could not comprehend Dawn Run getting beat, even though she had gone through 50 years of horses and knew how horses got beat and had always accepted it.' Paddy, also, has unpleasant memories of the aftermath of the race. He says, 'I can't describe the way Tony was ticked off that evening.'

Tony was to be jocked off once more and Jonjo, recovering from his injury, was called in for the Gold Cup. Jonjo travelled to Ireland to school Dawn Run around Gowran Park and Punchestown. The mare's lad, John Clarke, recalls how, shortly before Jonjo's arrival, he was involved in schooling Dawn Run across fences. He says, 'Paddy Mullins brought myself and Tony over to the farm at Closutton where his son Willy is living. There were two fences there like what you would find in Punchestown. I was riding Dawn Run and Tony was riding Pearlstone. The trainer says to jump the two fences, and I remember that Dawn Run pinged the two of them.'

Then Jonjo arrived at Doninga. He recalls how the schooling at Gowran Park went badly. 'I was wondering not just if she should have been favourite, but if she should even have been entered for the race,' he says. 'I schooled her again at Punchestown and this time Tony helped out by riding another horse around with us, and things went better on this occasion.' Few tipsters fancied Dawn Run as Gold Cup day came around. They were conscious of the mare's relative lack of experience as a 'chaser, her awkward performance at Cheltenham in January and the fact that Jonjo had never ridden her in a race over fences.

There was a huge media build-up to the Gold Cup and the Irish crowd at the Cheltenham Festival were on tenterhooks as the race got under way. Jonjo powered into the lead and kept in front for the first circuit, with only Run and Skip keeping up with the Irish partners. Then the two leading horses took the water jump. Dawn Run seemed to lose concentration, dropping her hind legs into the water with an enormous splash. Jim Murphy, head travelling lad with the mare on the day, says, 'I'm adamant that Dawn Run hurt herself sticking her hind legs in the water and that it was pure courage – and fitness – that kept her going. She was as fit as a flail. That was one thing a horse would never want for with Paddy Mullins – fitness. He had decades of experience at it.'

The spray thrown up by Dawn Run at the water jump momentarily blinded the goggles of Graham Bradley, following close behind on Wayward Lad. Dawn Run jumped awkwardly while taking the fifth fence from home and the Irish in the packed stands were dismayed to see the mare lose speed, while Run and Skip took up the lead. For several terrible moments Irish hearts skipped a beat as Dawn Run seemed to be getting 'beat'. But then, on the way down to the third last fence, it quickly became apparent that the mare was one of four horses still there with a chance, the others being Run and Skip, Wayward Lad and Forgive 'n' Forget.

At the final turn, Run and Skip was still leading with Wayward Lad closing, and Jonjo pulling out all the stops on the mare. Run and Skip's rider Steve Smith Eccles was to say later that he thought Dawn Run was beaten at that point, but the mare was made of sterner stuff. After rounding the turn, Jonjo asked the mare for all she had, and urged Dawn Run into taking the second last with an almighty jump. Run and Skip began to lose momentum, but the mare still had to contend with Wayward Lad and Forgive 'n' Forget who were still ahead of her. On the way up 'heartbreak hill', that killer of a hill that has taken the heart out of many a horse at the end of a hard-fought contest, the race was between Wayward Lad and Dawn Run, with the mare gradually gaining on her opponent.

With boots, whip and a supreme effort of will, Jonjo extracted a final surge from Dawn Run. Veteran commentator Peter O'Sullevan then called out the immortal words that were to throw all Ireland into ecstasy, 'The mare is beginning to get up!' To an almighty roar from the stands Dawn Run edged ahead and took the big prize by just a length. The first to shake Jonjo's hand was Wayward Lad's partner Graham Bradley, who was followed in this tribute by all the other riders in the race.

(Ironically, Jonjo had ridden Wayward Lad into third place in the Gold Cup in 1983.) Amid tumultuous scenes almost unprecedented in Cheltenham, a broadly grinning Jonjo punched the air in triumph as he was led into the unsaddling enclosure. An exuberant Jonjo remarked, 'Everyone thought the mare was beat – but nobody told her that!'

Tony Mullins recalls with a smile some of the funnier incidents during that time of incredible excitement in the enclosure. 'The crowd went crazy, and hundreds of people began to push towards the mare. The boss was getting annoyed and it began to look dangerous. There's a lad from up the road here in Gowran, Joe O'Riordan, a great old punter for years – his brother Pat owned Bermuda Classic. Joe is a helpful sort of fellow. The crowd was starting to push in on the mare and Joe puts out his two hands, and there are about 400 people coming and he says to the boss, "Don't worry, Paddy, I'll hold them back." And he was dead serious. And they stuck him to the railing.

'His brother Pat had arrived from Bermuda for the Gold Cup and he was also a great friend of Dawn Run. And in the excitement he had forgotten his parade ring pass so a big English policeman went to stop him at the gate and Pat says, "Now it's like this, you can let me in or you can come with me, but I'm f...g goin' in." The policeman let him in.' Tony went on, 'We were so confident of winning it, that half the celebrations went on during the three days leading up to the race. I just can't imagine what it would have been like had she got beat. I just could not see her beat. I was dumbfounded at the second last when she looked beat. I could not believe it, and I don't really know what happened. I would imagine that the mare didn't like getting a belt of the stick.'

CHAPTER 12

An Empty Feeling

Paddy Mullins had just pulled off the most historic win in his career – a win that will forever be remembered wherever followers of National Hunt racing are gathered, and whenever the history of the sport is recounted. The Master of Doninga well and truly entered the history books that day when Dawn Run became the only racehorse ever to win the Champion Hurdle and the Gold Cup. But while all Ireland rejoiced over Dawn Run's Gold Cup triumph, there was no feeling of celebration in the heart of the trainer who had done so much to bring sporting glory that day to his family, his stable and indeed his country. For Paddy Mullins and for his wife there was only a feeling of emptiness.

Paddy feels that he put his son Tony into the January race at Cheltenham to 'take the knocks' but was not able to put him into the big race, the Gold Cup, to reap the benefits of that earlier 'prep' run which had resulted in his son being unseated. Says Paddy, 'My feeling after the Gold Cup was one of absolute numbness. I would not have minded so badly only I had stuck Tony in to get a fall off the mare when schooling her around Cheltenham in preparation for the Gold Cup. That was the part that really got to me. I sacrificed him. Mrs Hill was only waiting for something to happen. We had done everything meticulously right. We had gone to the trouble of bringing the mare to Cheltenham in January to give her a school around the track and did the thing perfectly, including letting her have a belt off one of the fences. We paid the penalty and saw it materialise into a win in the Gold Cup, and I got little appreciation for doing that . . . I just did not feel like celebrating.'

Meanwhile, Mrs Hill also made it clear to Paddy that following the Gold Cup, Dawn Run would be going back to France for the Champion Hurdle. Says Paddy, 'She told me, "We're going back to France." And she said this despite the fact that I had stated on TV, while being interviewed in this very room [the drawing room at Doninga] that I did not think it would be a good thing to go for another run in the French Champion Hurdle. I felt that, as the mare had been schooled to jump over fences, she should not go back to jump over these little French hurdles. But Mrs Hill was determined to go back to France.'

Tony Mullins recalls clearly his own personal, and rather confused reaction to the Gold Cup victory. 'The day of the Gold Cup was a day of mixed emotions. The most disappointing thing in my life was not winning the Gold Cup on Dawn Run, but at the same time there was huge excitement at the yard winning the Gold Cup. It was a very confusing day. I was very excited over the win and still very sorry that I had not ridden the mare. I remember two reporters, and they must have been stalking me from behind. I was watching the race on the lawn that day, and as soon as the mare got up on the line, the first thing they did was to turn to me and ask me what did I think. I felt like hitting them but I just remarked, "My family has just won the Gold Cup – why wouldn't I be happy?" I left it at that. Maybe they were hoping for me to say something against Mrs Hill. That was certainly a confusing day. I still don't know if I was more happy or sad.

'As regards how my mother and father felt, it was a very awkward issue and I never brought it up. I knew that they wanted me to ride the horse, but basically we never spoke about it. I knew that if there was any possible way my father could get me back onto the mare he would have done it. It was hard enough, and there was enough pressure on, without bringing it up in conversation. On the day itself, I remember the funny part for me was Jonjo carrying me in on his shoulders up to the Queen Mother and I nearly falling in on top of her. You know how it is when you're getting down off a lad's shoulders. I nearly crashed into her. I remember the Queen Mother said something to me and I had not been expecting to be landed in front of her and I did not know at first what to say. But then I found it so easy to talk to her. Then one of the sponsors said something to me and I remember when I came up beside Mrs Hill she turned away to say something to someone else. Maybe she was embarrassed.' Jonjo, keenly aware of Tony's disappointment at not getting the ride on Dawn Run that day, tried, in his own unorthodox way, to console the jocked off rider. Carrying Tony into the winner's enclosure was Jonjo's way of trying to share some of the glory with him.

Tony's mother Maureen also has vivid memories of her meeting with the Queen Mother in the aftermath of the Gold Cup win, after the Queen Mother had presented the trophy to Mrs Hill. She also found the Queen Mother very easy to talk to. Says Maureen, 'The Queen Mother is an extraordinary person and her memory is incredible. She remarked that she recalled this particular horse coming down the hill and went on to describe a Gold Cup about 20 years previously. I remembered the race as she began to describe it. She was saying it was remarkable that mares rarely ran in it. She is terribly sharp and has an innate knowledge of National Hunt racing. She is absolutely dedicated to the sport and has done a lot for it. The Queen Mother knows a lot about the way racing is run and how hard working are the girls and chaps who look after the horses. She knows all about the routine of training that many owners would not know.'

Dawn Run's lad, John Clarke recalls how he was given a bottle of champagne after the win. When they had settled Dawn Run down in a stable, he and colleagues Jim Murphy and a stable jockey Peter Kavanagh went to the Cheltenham hostel canteen. 'All the lads from all the stables were there and we got a big cheer as we came in. We opened up the champagne and had a great celebration. Later that night we came back with the mare to Doninga. I remember coming home at about 5 o'clock in the morning and then cycling back to the stable at 8 o'clock for work. There were unbelievable celebrations in Bagenalstown and the other towns around. They brought the Gold Cup to one or two of the pubs, and also to Matty's in Royal Oak where I used to play pool. The Sunday after the win I was at Mass in the church at Bagenalstown, up in the gallery. The parish priest, Father Edward Dowling, spotted me in the gallery. Before the Mass started, he said from the altar, "I would like to say congratulations to John Clarke over the great triumph during the week." And they all started clapping. It was unbelievable, the reaction locally.'

Tony Mullins recalled how the Dawn Run saga affected his family. 'The Dawn Run situation was difficult for us to handle as a family. If a family has a problem they can discuss it and deal with it but it is very hard to deal with it with 60 million people reading about it in the newspapers every day. We had a working relationship and a family relationship, and you really have to be in that situation to see how difficult it is. It was one of the big sports stories of the time. It was like a rumbling volcano there the whole time, and we all did our best simply to avoid it, and I'd say it was never discussed within the family. It was a very hard thing to talk about. I would imagine that my father always wonders should he have put his foot down, because I do believe, without praising myself, that the mare ran better for me than she did for anybody.

'But then what would be the reaction if I fell off her at the top of the hill again – and it could happen. After all, she fell at the first with Jonjo in her next race after the Gold Cup. If I had fallen off her the whole of Europe would say that Paddy Mullins, as a trainer, had made the wrong decision. And they would say he had made the wrong decision for family reasons, that he had lost himself in his family. As a professional man he was in a very difficult situation. It was awkward because most of us were all together at home at the time. We were living and working together. I'd say that Dawn Run was never, ever discussed really in the house.'

For Irish racegoers, it was a great Cheltenham Festival. Not only had Dawn Run won the Gold Cup, but the mare's old Irish adversary, the Michael 'Mouse' Morris-trained gelding Buck House, won the Queen Mother Champion Chase, outclassing, among others, Very Promising and Bobsline. But the uncertainty that surrounds the business of racing was underlined in a dramatic way during the month after Cheltenham. Fresh from their Gold Cup triumph, Jonjo was partnering Dawn Run in the Whitbread Gold Label Cup at Liverpool on 3 April when the mare fell at the first fence. Mrs Hill was disappointed but said little to Paddy Mullins about the setback. Paddy got the impression that her attitude was that if only she had been riding, the mare would not have fallen! Meanwhile, back in Ireland, a special race was organised at Paddy Mullins's local racecourse, Gowran Park, in honour of Dawn Run, and it was envisaged that the mare would be making a 'guest appearance' and taking part. Unfortunately, the race was arranged at short notice and details were not in the official calendar but on a separate sheet of paper. This led to a misunderstanding at Doninga and the end result was that the entries closed, and Dawn Run was not in the race. Mrs Hill was furious.

It is not generally known that the trainer Vincent O'Brien helped to set the ball rolling for another race in honour of the mare – the match with the mare's old rival Buck House that was to be held in front of an excited, capacity crowd at Punchestown on 23 April. According to Paddy, the match helped to assuage Mrs Hill's anger over the mare missing out on the special race at Gowran. Recalls Tony Mullins, 'It was Vincent O'Brien who dreamed up the match. We were all saying what a pity it was that the mare was going to miss the race at Gowran and Dr O'Brien approached me. I think we were at the Lincoln meeting at The Curragh. He tapped me on the shoulder – I had never been speaking to him but often nodded to him – and said, "If we organised a match do you think your father would run Dawn Run in it?" I said, "I'm sure he will." Dr O'Brien's involvement in the match was never really made

public.' Somebody asked Tony would they need a pacemaker –
i.e. a third horse to take part in the race. Tony replied jauntily
that if they so desired they could fit a pacemaker into Buck
House but Dawn Run didn't need one.

The huge crowd at Punchestown was vibrant with
excitement as Dawn Run and Buck House set off on the two
mile race, at level weights, with £20,000 at stake. Tony had
been re-united with Dawn Run for the occasion and Tommy
Carmody was on Buck House, which was owned by Mrs Phil
Purcell, a sister of a former Kerry football star of the 1950s,
Micksie Palmer. Tommy Carmody encouraged Buck House in a
dramatic leap at the third last which gave him an advantage and
he still had the advantage at the second last. But when Tony
called on the mare for some last-minute favours she didn't
disappoint him and Dawn Run won convincingly by two and a
half lengths. The mare got a rapturous reception from the
crowd as she was led into the winner's enclosure.

Tony considers that the mare's proud, independent spirit
was particularly in evidence during this race. He recalls, 'Buck
House came up beside the mare at the second last, and I
reckoned there was a fair race going on, and I said to myself we
are not going to win this on the bridle, and I pulled out the stick
to give her one. But when my hand moved and she saw the stick
she stopped so quickly I nearly went up on her ears. If you
watch the video you can see me putting down the stick again
and I rode hands and heels and she flew. She wasn't going to
take what she got in the Gold Cup – from anyone. I have no
doubt about that. It wasn't that she was dishonest but she
wasn't going to let anyone do that to her. It wasn't Jonjo's fault
on the day – he had to do it.'

In June that year, Dawn Run returned to France once more
to compete in the Prix La Barka, the 'prep' race for the French
Champion Hurdle. Tony was the rider. The mare had won this
race easily with Tony up two years previously but this time all
the duo could manage was to come second to the formidable Le
Rheusois. Tony recalls, 'I said to the boss after we came in – if
we come back again we are going to get beat – we will never

beat this horse, Le Rheusois. Mrs Hill turned to my father as I turned to go away and she said, "If he hasn't the confidence to ride her to win we will get somebody who has." I remember an hour or two later, waiting for the taxi, he said to her, "I don't want to come back. I think that Tony is right, this horse will beat us for speed" and she said, "There is good prize money for second, we will come back." He never argued any more and he just trained the mare on for it but at no stage did he ever want to go back.'

Dawn Run wins the Cheltenham Gold Cup, March 1986, two years after her victory in the Champion Hurdle.

(GERRY CRANHAM)

Tony on Dawn Run (left) *and Tommy Carmody on Buck House*
before the famous 'Match' at Punchestown on 23 April 1986.

Pictured at a reception to announce Paddy as Champion
National Hunt trainer were (left to right): *Vincent O'Brien,*
Maureen, Jacqueline O'Brien and Paddy.

Princess Anne greets the late Mrs Charmian Hill (back to camera) and Paddy during the ceremony to mark the unveiling of the statue to Dawn Run at Cheltenham.

After the first of his two successive wins in Europe's richest handicap hurdle, Redundant Pal with his winning owners (left to right): Sean Boyne, Tim O'Connor, Peter O'Neill, Gerard Cooke and Jimmy Magee. Leopardstown, 14 January 1989. (LIAM HEALY)

Dueling Grounds
Race Course
April 22, 1990

GRABEL
$750,000 DUELING GROUNDS
INTERNATIONAL HURDLE STAKES

Owners: P. Kehoe & Mrs. P. M
Trainer: Patrick Mullins
Jockey: Tony Mullins

Photos by Anne M. Eberhardt

*A cutting from an American racing magazine chronicling
Grabel's famous victory in the Dueling Grounds on 22 April
1990.*

Adrian Maguire drives The Gooser to victory in the Galway Plate on 29 July 1992. (LIAM HEALY)

Mrs Margaret O'Leary, owner of The Gooser, receives the Galway Plate from Lord Hemphill after Adrian Maguire had ridden him to victory on 29 July 1992. Also pictured (left to right) Luke Mullins (Paddy's brother, manager of the Galway track), the late Tom O'Leary, Adrian Maguire, Paddy and Maureen. (LIAM HEALY)

Paddy on the gallops at Doninga – with Tony Treacy on Royal Albert. (SEAN BOYNE)

Returning to the stables after work on the Doninga gallops.
(SEAN BOYNE)

The Master of Doninga explains a point to Tony Treacy.
(SEAN BOYNE)

Examining one of his horses in the yard.
(SEAN BOYNE)

Paddy and Maureen with in the background (left to right): *Sandra, George, Margaret (Tony's wife), Tony, Willy, Jackie (Willy's wife), Peter McCarthy (Sandra's husband) and Tom.*
(CAROLINE NORRIS)

The Master of Doninga. (LIAM O'CONNOR)

CHAPTER 13

Death in Paris

It was a baking hot day in Paris when the gallant Dawn Run went out to do battle for the last time. The date will be etched forever in the memory of those who were close to the mare – 27 June 1986. Mrs Hill didn't want to send Tony to ride the mare in this second attempt at the French Champion Hurdle, known in French as the Grand Course de Haies. Paddy Mullins, who had grave misgivings about sending the mare back out over hurdles when she had been schooled for fences, engaged a French jockey, the veteran 41-year-old Michel Chirol, to partner Dawn Run in the race at Auteuil. There appeared to be an omen of what was to happen when Gaye Brief, ridden by Peter Scudamore, took a tumble at the schooling hurdle on the way to the start. Gaye Brief was to take another fall during the race itself. The horse somersaulted on top of the rider's legs and Scudamore counts himself lucky that they were not broken.

Meanwhile, Chirol seemed to have Dawn Run in top gear and was making ground relentlessly along the inner when disaster struck at the fifth last. The big mare barely took off and had a headlong fall. The horse that Tony feared the mare would not beat, Le Rheusois, went on to cross the line five lengths ahead of the American challenger Flatterer, ridden by Richard Dunwoody. The favourite, Gacko, was two lengths away third, and the other two local horses also completed the course. Dunwoody described the heat on the course as 'unreal' – the hottest he ever had to contend with.

Meanwhile, many pairs of binoculars scanned the fifth last where the Irish mare lay motionless on the ground. Course staff were frantically signalling for veterinary assistance and a horse ambulance accelerated across the infield to where Dawn Run lay. Chirol, however, knew instinctively when he looked behind him after the fall that Dawn Run was beyond assistance. She had died instantly from a broken neck. Chirol said later through an interpreter that they were just about to accelerate but the mare never lifted.

The travelling head lad in the Mullins stable, Jim Murphy was watching the race from the stand and became anxious when Dawn Run did not reappear after her fall. He made his way across to where she lay. 'She was either dying or dead,' he recalls. 'Paddy Mullins came over as well. The saddle was already gone – the jockey would probably have taken that. I took the only things that you could take off her – the shin boots and the bridle. That was all that was left to come home. Chirol the jockey was devastated. He was the man for that race. He had a load of experience and was very, very good. The French loved him. I tried to get the mare's passport. There were a lot of stamps in it – the pages were almost full. I was with the mare on almost all of her trips out of Ireland, and her passport was a thing I would have loved to have got. But I couldn't get it. I presume it was held in France. So the last time I saw Dawn Run was as she was lying by the second hurdle up the back straight at Auteuil. I did not see the carcase being taken away. I came back with the boss to the enclosure and saw no more of the mare.'

As a crestfallen Paddy Mullins, death certificate in hand, returned with Jim Murphy to the enclosure, they were approached by members of the media. Paddy was quoted as saying at the time, 'A tragedy, but the less said about it the better.' Jim was quoted as saying simply, 'It's a shame.' Whatever Mrs Hill may have been thinking, she showed no outward sign of emotion. Her only comment to Paddy Mullins was, 'Horses come and horses go.' Says Paddy, 'Her attitude was to get on with the next horse. She was a tough woman.'

However, she did want to view the body of the mare, and became very angry and protested strongly when she found the carcase had been taken away before she could see it. The day was very hot and the racecourse authorities wanted to get the carcase away to the abattoir as soon as possible. Was Mrs Hill simply asserting her rights? Or was there, beneath her tough exterior, some stirring of sentiment which impelled her to view the body of Dawn Run one last time before it disappeared forever?

Paddy Mullins's reservations about sending the mare to race in the French Champion Hurdle proved to have been well-founded after all. As he came in to the bar at Auteuil for a drink with Mrs Hill after the race, somebody said to him, 'You were right.' It was the second tragedy to hit Irish National Hunt racing within a few weeks. The death of Dawn Run was preceded by that of her great rival Buck House, who died from colic in a field in Tipperary.

Tony Mullins will always remember how, where and when he got the bad news about the mare. 'When Dawn Run was killed, I will never forget it. I was in Dublin, at the Ballsbridge Sales, where the Derby Sales were on, and a phone call came in to say that Dawn Run fell, and I laughed, and said, "It's good enough for her, I'll get back on her next season." About ten minutes later somebody said she is dead. I just could not believe it. I had imagined her getting beat, or going on the wrong track or running away with the French jockey, but I could never imagine her getting killed, and I felt I had thought of every angle before she went to France. My father did not want to send her, and of course Mrs Hill did not want to send me.

'I can imagine how the end came about. The thing about the mare is that she was not the fastest of all time. But if ever a horse was getting to her she would let fly at a hurdle and that would sicken the horse beside her, and then she would get a chance on the Flat and let fly at the next and eventually she would wear the other animal down. But this day in France, when they quickened going down the back she let fly at one and she only got a half length on them. She was on top of her

163

head going down to the next and she let fly again and she only got the half length and she was used to getting three lengths. Then she goes down to the next and says to herself, "I'm not going to let them get away with this" and she lets fly so far from the hurdle she catches the top of it coming down, and that's what happened. At least that's the way I would imagine it happened.'

Jonjo O'Neill was also at the Ballsbridge Sales when word came through about the death of Dawn Run. A shell-shocked Jonjo told the *Racing Post*, 'My lasting memory of Dawn Run will be the mare who was never beat. She was so tough and courageous you could never count her out of a race.' Jonjo went on, 'She was as tough as old boots but what a character when you were on her back. She needed humouring and, like most women, wanted to do things her way and in her own time. You couldn't tell her what to do. She was a great challenge for any jockey to ride . . . ' Close on a decade on, Jonjo can still recall his shock of hearing about the mare's death. He remembers meeting up with Tony Mullins soon after the bad news came through and discussing it with him. 'We were both very glad that we were not riding the mare when she was killed,' he says. Looking back on his relationship with the mare, he remarks, 'Dawn Run was difficult to ride. I think she used to run better for Tony than she did for me! But we got her motivated on the day. Sure that was the main thing.'

John Clarke, the lad who always looked after Dawn Run, could not go to France as he had hurt his knee playing football. It was the only one of the mare's overseas expeditions on which he did not travel. He went to a bookmaker's shop in Carlow to listen to the commentary and heard how Dawn Run fell – and that was all. He returned to the Mullins yard and, about ten minutes before the 5 p.m. 'knocking off' time an unconfirmed rumour swept around the yard that Dawn Run was dead. But it was not until he tuned in to a TV news bulletin at home later that evening that the ominous rumour was confirmed – Dawn Run had been killed. He recalls, 'I was devastated. I cried like a baby. And then not being there. I had wanted to be there. Oh,

Jaysus, I'll never forget it. Mrs Hill was around afterwards – she was dumbstruck.'

In Ireland and in Britain, the death of Dawn Run was treated by the media with all the solemnity normally accorded to the demise of a rock superstar, or a statesman or a prince of the church. There were front page news stories, obituaries, colour pieces, and BBC TV even broadcast a special tribute to the dead mare. All that was lacking was a funeral. Letters and messages of sympathy flowed into the Mullins household from many parts of the world. At home in Ireland, there was also some resentment over the death of the mare. There had been few Irish racing superstars since Arkle and some people felt aggrieved that a heroine of the turf had been taken away from them. Some commentators suggested that the mare had died because of Mrs Hill's relentless pursuit of prize money.

But Paddy Mullins here comes stoutly to the defence of his late client. 'Mrs Hill was never greedy,' he says with conviction. He points out also that she could have made a lot of money by selling Dawn Run and this would undoubtedly have meant the mare going abroad. But the question of parting with the mare never entered her mind for a moment, despite some very tempting offers, he says. Paddy reckons that at the height of her career, Dawn Run could have fetched a quarter of a million pounds.

Tony Mullins can remember the tension that arose from the Dawn Run saga – but, reminiscing about the mare and the impact she had on his family, he can also remember the lighter moments. One particular incident stands out in his mind. He recalls, 'We were sitting at home one night, and as you know my father checks over the horses at midnight. We had come back from an evening meeting and we were talking about the day's events. The next thing, through the kitchen window, I could see him coming and I knew by his walk there was something wrong. "Oh God," I said to myself, "is Dawn Run hurt or is there something wrong? Has she a leg?" I said to the other lads, "He's coming in and there's something wrong."

'He comes in anyway and everyone goes quiet. He had his

own special wheelbarrow for feeding the horses in the night. And he announces, "My wheelbarrow is punctured." We all started to laugh. We were so relieved. And he says, "I'm glad ye find it so funny" and goes back out again. It was hilarious. We were all imagining that the mare was hurt.' One of the lighter moments that Paddy Mullins himself recalls was when Dawn Run ran at Kempton. Mrs Hill's son Oliver came into the paddock and started giving instructions to Jonjo O'Neill. Jonjo tried to keep a straight face – he was already talking to the owner and trainer of the horse he was about to mount. Oliver had got his races mixed up. Paddy recalls, 'Jonjo came back into the paddock from the race roaring laughing.'

The head travelling lad with the mare, Jim Murphy, recalls how they mounted a night watch on Dawn Run at Doninga the week before the Champion Hurdle. 'It was a tense time and because she was such a hot favourite she was kept under constant watch. We took it in turns to stay up all night – two people would sit in a car in the yard.' Then the mare was taken over on the ferry to Matt Delahooke's stables near Cheltenham. The lads stayed up all night to keep watch on the mare at the Delahooke stables. A friend of the Mullins family, Pat O'Riordan, owner of Bermuda Classic, helped out by staying up part of the night. Then, in the morning, the lads had to exercise other horses and were away for a couple of hours, and Dawn Run was left on her own. Jim recalls with amusement Delahooke's comment to them when they got back to the stables. 'He said to us, "Typical Irish – mind her all night and then go away and leave her." How right he was!'

Charmian Hill and Paddy Mullins were each strong-willed and highly individualistic. Each had definite views, and unfortunately those views sometimes diverged. But despite the differences between owner and trainer, there was always a mutual respect between them. Despite the disagreements, Mrs Hill always left Dawn Run at Doninga, even though she could easily have sent the mare to another stable. She told reporters before Dawn Run took part in the Champion Hurdle that Paddy was a marvellous trainer, the best anyone could have, and there is no reason to believe that she did not mean it. Mrs Hill was not the type for flattery or insincere compliments. Paddy, for his part, says that despite their differences, Mrs Hill was one of the best customers a trainer could have. 'She was the tops,' he says.

Probably, as regards the world of racing, one of the worst days in the life of the two of them was when Dawn Run was killed. One can only guess at what the mare might have achieved had she lived – some observers believe she could have won another couple of Gold Cups. Yet there was to be some consolation for owner and trainer later that same year when Mrs Hill's Boro Quarter won the Galway Plate. The mare had been bred by Mrs Hill and it was the first time that Paddy had won the premier event at Galway. Mrs Hill had brought Boro Quarter as a filly to the Mullins stable in 1984. After winning several races over hurdles and on the Flat, Boro Quarter recorded her first win over fences when Tony Mullins rode her to victory in a novice 'chase at Clonmel in December 1985. She notched up a couple more wins over fences.

Then came her crowning glory when, on 30 July 1986, with Peter Kavanagh riding, she took the Galway Plate. During the race, Shuil Liss looked to be going best of all, but when she fell at the third last fence, the main danger to Boro Quarter was removed. Boro Quarter won with Bold Agent four lengths behind and Winning Nora staying on to take third place. An overjoyed Mrs Hill was so overcome that she actually kissed Paddy Mullins in the parade ring. Says Paddy, 'It was a nice gesture.' Meanwhile, there was a bizarre incident when the Gold Cup was reported stolen from Mrs Hill's Waterford home. The gardai were called in and the cup was discovered – it emerged that somebody had put the trophy into a chest in the house for safekeeping.

During the Cheltenham Festival in 1987, a statue in honour of Dawn Run was unveiled at the racecourse where the mare had covered herself in glory. It was financed by public subscription to a fund organised by the *Racing Post*. Princess Anne performed the unveiling and she chatted to Paddy

Mullins, telling how she loved to ride but did not get enough time. The man from Doninga had some horses over for the festival and there and then invited her to ride out any of them the following morning. The Princess regretfully had to decline the offer. Paddy had seen the Princess ride in cross country events on TV and regards her as a fine horsewoman. Among those present for the unveiling was Dawn Run's owner.

Mrs Hill continued riding out at Doninga – until disaster struck. Paddy Mullins was away one day attending a meeting. He was a committee member for many years of the Irish Trainers Association and had gone to The Curragh to represent the ITA at a meeting there. While he was away, Mrs Hill was injured in a fall off her own mare, Boro Quarter, who had won the Galway Plate. Paddy says, 'I feel that if I had been home that day, the accident would not have happened. I would not have allowed Mrs Hill to do what she was doing. She was riding Boro Quarter around a gallop and the animal was a bit strong for her. She was so tired she fell off. Tom was the only one here that day and he said he could not stop her.'

Jim Murphy, who had been with Dawn Run on so many of her trips abroad, was on the gallops when the accident happened. He recalls, 'Her leg was at an angle – clearly broken. She said she would be all right. We all patched her up as best we could and she was put into the ambulance. I can still picture her on the ground, with jodhpurs and a little red jumper – she wasn't eight stone weight. You felt you could almost pick her up and put her under your arm. She was really tough. She was probably numb as she lay on the ground. I think the local GP attended her first. We all stayed by her. The riding out stopped. I think that was the last time she rode out. She normally rode most of her own. She rode Dawn Run an awful lot. I liked her. I thought she was a very straight person. In her, we had the Anne Duchess of Westminster of Irish racing. Just as the Duchess would not sell Arkle, Mrs Hill would not sell Dawn Run. Most other people, the weight of money offered would have encouraged them to sell.'

Paddy Mullins gave up committee work after Mrs Hill's

accident, because of his concern that he might have prevented it had he been present that day. He recalls going to see Mrs Hill in hospital, where she was to spend several weeks. She had smashed her hip in the fall and seemed very low. He suspects it was the beginning of her physical decline. She subsequently suffered a stroke and died in 1990. And what of the other players in the Dawn Run drama? Tony Mullins, well established now as a trainer, says from his base in Gowran, 'My regret is that I never won the Gold Cup, and never had a winner at the Cheltenham Festival. I certainly rode horses that were capable of doing it. I did nearly everything else I wanted to do, like winning the French Champion Hurdle, which no Irish or British jockey had ever done. I was champion jockey riding over hurdles only, which nobody had ever done. I was leading rider at Aintree. And I won the richest jump race in the world, in America in 1990 with Grabel. So I got everything, except the big one in Cheltenham. But I am quite happy with my career, and if I were doing it again I would be happy with the same. I would be very happy to get near it in training.'

Jonjo O'Neill suffered his own share of tragedy. The jockey who endeared himself to the racegoing public by his sheer good humour and ebullient high spirits, retired from riding to train at his Ivy House Farm near Penrith. Soon he was diagnosed as suffering from cancer of the lymph glands. With great courage he overcame the cancer – only to undergo the trauma of a difficult divorce from his wife Sheila, mother of his three children. His training career is going well. At the Cheltenham Festival of 1995, he saddled Front Line, winner of the National Hunt Chase, for Irish owner J.P. McManus, the high-rolling gambler who has been dubbed Ireland's 'Prince of Punters'. Jonjo will never forget his ride to victory on Dawn Run in the Gold Cup. 'It was the highlight of my career,' he says now, almost a decade on. And his memories of Paddy Mullins are easy to summarise – 'a quiet man, and a brilliant trainer'.

Jim Murphy, who travelled with Dawn Run on most of her trips abroad, set up in the bloodstock business himself, and runs a very successful stud farm near Goresbridge. He is married with one son. John Clarke, the lad who looked after Dawn Run, married a girl he used to meet while cycling through Royal Oak on his way from work at Doninga. He did well on a management course with the bookmakers William Hill in London, and worked with the organisation for a number of years before returning to his native Bagenalstown, where he lives with his wife and two children. He misses being involved with the horses at Doninga and he still has a number of mementos of Dawn Run, which he keeps in a big cardboard box. They are among his most treasured possessions. Michel Chirol, the last man to ride Dawn Run, is retired from racing and runs a successful restaurant in the South of France.

Paddy Mullins was at a race meeting in Punchestown when the death of Mrs Hill was announced to the crowds over the public address system. He had heard about the death shortly before it was made public. Mrs Hill's son Jeremy had a very fine horse with Paddy Mullins, Boro Eight, until it was sold to another owner. Says Paddy of Jeremy, 'He was always a very understanding owner, and the nicest man you could meet.' During the glittering career of Dawn Run, the mare had record first-prize earnings over jumps of £269,083. She ran 35 times between 1982 and 1986, winning 21 races. She set up a new record time for the Champion Hurdle of 3 min 52.6 and for the Gold Cup of 6 min 35.3. Mrs Hill's mare had only two falls – at the first fence in Liverpool, and at Auteuil, the tragic fall that ended her life, and her great career. The likes of such a formidable duo – mare and owner – will not be seen again for a very long time.

CHAPTER 14

A Row over 'The Pal'

Few horses have had the distinction of figuring in a Parliamentary debate but one such animal is Redundant Pal, one of the better horses in the Mullins yard in the 1980s and early 1990s. Owned by a partnership mainly composed of Dublin journalists, Redundant Pal won Europe's richest handicap hurdle race, the Ladbroke, two years in a row in 1989 and 1990. The connections did not really expect Redundant Pal to win for the second successive year, so when 'The Pal' as he was affectionately known by his owners, thundered first past the winning post, their joy knew no bounds. The win led to some controversy, and to Redundant Pal being mentioned in a debate in the Dail. But even this development could not seriously detract from the owners' satisfaction of winning this big race two years in a row.

As Redundant Pal was being led into the winner's enclosure at Leopardstown following his second Ladbroke victory, one or two angry punters called out, 'What about the two horse race?' This was a reference to the S. M. Morris Hurdle the previous month at Leopardstown featuring only Redundant Pal and Firion's Law. Redundant Pal was fancied to win but Firion's Law, considered a much inferior horse at the time, won the match easily. It appeared to some of the sceptics that there had been a dramatic, and inexplicable, improvement in Redundant Pal's form which allowed him to go on and win the Ladbroke. Paddy Mullins was brought before the stewards to explain the improvement in form. He said he could not explain what happened, and the stewards accepted his word.

Brendan McGahon, a Fine Gael TD (Member of Parliament) raised the question of Redundant Pal during a Budget debate in the Dail (Irish Parliament). Some pundits think it was the first time that a racehorse had figured in a Dail debate in this way since a row over the purchase of Tulyar by the state-run National Stud back in the 1950s. Speaking under parliamentary privilege, Mr McGahon said, 'Every punter in Ireland, except a chosen few, mistrusts Irish racing and not without cause. The racing industry should be the subject of a national inquiry and this mistrust is the key reason why attendances are dwindling in Ireland; why the man in the street is gambling on English racing and in some cases gambling on racing in Happy Valley in Hong Kong. *Fiddler on the Roof* was the name of a top musical some years ago. Fiddlers on the Hoof would be an apt description of the Irish racing scene.

'The final indignity for punters was the incredible Redundant Pal story at Christmas. On the Friday at Leopardstown, an animal named Firion's Law was beaten three-quarters of a length by Scally Owen – a reversal of 24 lengths on their previous running. Twenty-four hours later, Redundant Pal, a stablemate of Scally Owen and a vastly superior horse to Scally Owen, is beaten at 1/5 by Firion's Law. Three weeks later, Redundant Pal wins a £25,000 hurdle with Firion's Law 42 lengths behind – almost two parishes away. Is it any wonder that the crowds are staying away in such numbers? I do not believe the Holy Ghost knows what is happening in Irish racing. While I know an owner does not pay expensive rates for the benefit of the public, the Racing Board and the Turf Club must strike a balance if the image of Irish racing is to improve.'

Other commentators also called into question the performance of Redundant Pal, although in rather more restrained terms since they did not have the kind of parliamentary privilege enjoyed by Mr McGahon. The debate was carried on in the press and on the radio. Some punters even booed the Mullins horse Scally Owen at Punchestown. Paddy Mullins kept a dignified silence throughout, although he was annoyed at some of the comment which he describes as 'vitriolic'. 'What annoyed me more than anything else was McGahon who got up in the Dail and made those comments,' he says. Paddy was also amazed at the ill-informed nature of some of the comments made during the controversy. 'Some people tried to make out that by losing the match with Firion's Law, Redundant Pal was in a better position in the weights to win the Ladbroke,' he says. 'In fact Redundant Pal wasn't going to get a pound more for winning the match. Beating Firion's Law would have made no difference at all to the weights.'

Paddy reckons that part of the problem is that people did not realise how good a horse Firion's Law was at the time. 'They thought Firion's Law was a complete and utter dodo, which he wasn't at all.' Firion's Law went on to prove himself to be a very superior racehorse winning, among other races, the prestigious Galway Plate. One commentator, John Comyn, writing in the *Evening Herald* in November 1991, referred to the consistency of the record of Firion's Law, and recalled how he first came to prominence when he beat Redundant Pal in the two-horse race of December 1989. Comyn goes on, 'Perhaps we were all wrong in our assessment of that race at that time. Firion's Law has gone on to win many excellent races, including this year's Galway Plate. As things stand, he could yet be a Gold Cup horse . . . '

During the Redundant Pal controversy, Paddy Mullins received the backing of supporters and well-wishers. The trainer Vincent O'Brien and his wife Jacqueline sent a message expressing sorrow over the unfounded criticism, adding, 'Do not worry, it will pass.' An old friend, eye specialist Everard Hewson who lives at Craughwell, Co. Galway, wrote to the *Irish Field* in defence of the Mullins family. Explaining that he had known the family for many years, and had the pleasure of riding out 'under the instructions of the Master of Doninga, his wife and children', Hewson went on to say that he never heard even the slightest suggestion of underhand practice or underhand tactics at the stable. He went on, 'Never have I known a horse from Doninga to run on other than on merit.'

Redundant Pal was a sign of a new era in Irish racing – the era of the horse that is owned by a group of people – either a partnership (five owners or less) or a syndicate (more than five owners). The Dublin-based partnership that owned Redundant Pal consisted of Tim O'Connor, head of TV Sport at RTE, Ireland's national broadcasting station; leading sports commentator and columnist Jimmy Magee; finance company executive Gerard Cooke and the two co-authors of this book, journalists Sean Boyne and Peter O'Neill. The horse ran in the colours of Peter O'Neill, who had previously headed another partnership that owned Boreen Rambler, who was also trained by Paddy Mullins.

Ironically, one of those who originally had the idea to acquire Redundant Pal was Frank Richardson, a high-flying senior executive with the Coyle Hamilton insurance company. But Frank had to drop out of the deal and his place in the partnership was taken by a friend Gerard Cooke. Frank, a keen racing fan and punter, later joined a seminary as a late vocation and is now a priest in America. After Redundant Pal's second Ladbroke win, one of Frank's pals was quoted in a newspaper thus, 'Frank switched from horses to Heaven. It was a case of holy orders instead of under orders.'

Redundant Pal proved to be an excellent servant for the five-man partnership that owned him, winning for them a total of more than £150,000 in prize money before being sold to an owner in England in 1992. He won a total of 13 races while owned by the partnership – on the Flat, over hurdles and over fences. Ironically, Paddy Mullins had been doubtful about entering him for his first Ladbroke in 1989, thinking the horse would have a much better chance of winning another race at the same Leopardstown meeting, the Fitzpatrick Castle Hurdle. But the owners had already backed him ante-post at 20–1 in the Ladbroke, and asked that he get a run in the race. Tony Mullins felt he never got on with Redundant Pal, and he opted to ride Derrymore Boy, while stable jockey Peter Kavanagh was assigned 'The Pal'.

Kavanagh gave the horse an excellent ride on the day. At the second last, one of the English challengers, Cashew King, executed a great jump and seemed to be going very well. However Atteses, ridden by Charlie Swan, was making good progress, tracked by Kingsmill, the 7–1 favourite. Redundant Pal overcame a last flight blunder to take the race by two lengths ahead of Atteses, with Kingsmill third. It was Paddy Mullins's first win in the event, formerly known as the Sweeps Hurdle. Says Paddy, 'It is a terribly difficult race to win. You need to have the horse handicapped to win it to start off with, and you also need all the luck in the world as well.'

Peter Kavanagh had been riding out for Paddy Mullins for the previous 15 years. Although easygoing and unassuming by nature, in the saddle he is known as a tough, determined rider. At this stage in his career he had been notching up a fair share of significant wins. He had ridden Boro Quarter to victory in the 1986 Galway Plate and at the Christmas Leopardstown meeting prior to his Ladbroke win he had ridden 6–1 chance Derrinore to take first place in the Denny Juvenile Hurdle. Around the time of his Ladbroke win a rather odd rumour went around that Kavanagh had always wanted to be an actor, and was deeply involved in amateur dramatics. The rumour even surfaced in the media. There was no basis whatever for the story, and Kavanagh was mystified as to how it got started. Meanwhile, the owners of Redundant Pal were more than happy to have Kavanagh to continue partnering the horse, but he was injured in a fall and was to spend a lengthy period in hospital. Paddy Mullins had to look around for another jockey.

The following year Redundant Pal was again entered for the Ladbroke, this time with the talented young Wexford-born rider Conor O'Dwyer in the saddle. The night before the race, Tim O'Connor, one of the owners of Redundant Pal, was at a dinner in Dublin hosted by the sponsors, Ladbrokes. He found himself seated beside trainer Jenny Pitman, whose charge Dis

Train, ridden by her son Mark, would also be taking part in the race next day. Mrs Pitman later told how Tim had correctly predicted the result of the race. He told her that Redundant Pal would be first, and Dis Train second.

It was the first time for Conor O'Dwyer to ride Redundant Pal, but he handled the horse exactly right on the day. The 4–1 favourite Fragrant Dawn was going well in the lead approaching the final turn, but Dis Train jumped the last in front and Mark Pitman seemed to have victory almost within his grasp. However, Conor O'Dwyer, timing his challenge to perfection, got a good final burst of speed out of Redundant Pal on the flat, going on to win by half a length from Dis Train, with Fragrant Dawn three lengths back in third and Joyful Noise fourth. The fact that Redundant Pal was carrying 19lb more on his back than in the previous Ladbroke made the victory all the sweeter for the connections.

Redundant Pal was to make a smooth transition to fences later that year. Ridden by Conor O'Dwyer, he had an easy win at 4–1 in the Irish National Hunt Novice Chase at Navan in October, beating the favourite Joyful Noise by four lengths. The following month, however, he showed the darker side of his Jekyll and Hyde character by trailing in fourth of five finishers in the INH Novice Chase Series at Tipperary. Then, in line with his unpredictability, Redundant Pal won the Novice Chase Championship at Punchestown in December.

At the Cheltenham Festival the following March, Redundant Pal took on some formidable two mile 'chasers, coming third in the Arkle Challenge Trophy behind Remittance Man and Uncle Ernie. A few weeks later, Redundant Pal was back in fighting form when he and another Irish-trained contender, Blitzkrieg, dominated the proceedings in the Captain Morgan Handicap Chase at the April meeting in Aintree. The Eddie O'Grady-trained Blitzkrieg, owned by high-rolling gambler J. P. McManus and ridden by Tommy Carmody, just got the better of his rival to win by one and a half lengths. After a lengthy stewards' inquiry, Blitzkrieg was confirmed as the winner. Early the following year, 1992, 'The

Pal' won two 'chases, including the valuable P. Z. Mower Chase at Thurles. At the Cheltenham Festival that year he put in one of his best performances ever, coming fourth behind Remittance Man, Katabatic and Waterloo Boy in a Queen Mother Champion Chase that was described as one of the best in years. In April 1992, Redundant Pal made it lucky thirteen for his owners when he won his 13th race, scoring an easy victory in the Oliver Freaney, Dan Moore Handicap Chase at Fairyhouse. Later in the year he was sold to the Martyn Meade stable in Wiltshire.

After Redundant Pal 'emigrated' to England, he never seemed to be the same force again. Looking back on the horse's career, what does Paddy Mullins think of him? 'Brilliant in patches, but unpredictable,' he says. 'When he let himself down to run, he could run. He would have had a lot of speed on the dam side of his family. His dam Palesa was by Palestine, and Palestine was a brilliant racehorse, the Aga Khan's best. Redundant Pal could be brilliant – the problem was predicting when he was going to be brilliant . . . '

* * *

Christy Maye was at the races in Fairyhouse one day in April 1986 and was fed up to see his mare Stringfellows beaten easily in a bumper by another horse. The wealthy hotelier from the Irish midlands was most impressed by the winner of the race on the day – and reckoned that if he was going to be really serious about winning races, this was the horse to do it. So he resolved there and then to buy the horse that had just beaten his own mare by some incredible number of lengths. And that was the beginning of the process whereby Cloughtaney came to the Mullins yard. The horse was to prove one of the best horses to be trained by Paddy Mullins in the late 1980s and early 1990s. And for owner Christy Maye, owner of the Greville Arms Hotel in Mullingar and the Bridge House Hotel, Tullamore, it was to provide great excitement and a marvellous series of wins, with prize money totalling more than £100,000.

Cloughtaney had been owned – and trained – by a Co. Tipperary farmer and cattle dealer, Eddie Hayden, who lives at Drangan, in the Mullinahone area. The popular farmer and horseman was in the news in 1995 when neighbours banded together to campaign against moves by a bank to seize his farm. He finally managed to work out a deal with the bank. Eddie remembers well how another deal was done – the deal to sell Cloughtaney. 'I got a phone call from Christy Maye, asking me if Cloughtaney was for sale, and then he and Paddy Mullins called down to see the horse. After looking at Cloughtaney, Paddy said he would like to train him. I remember Christy asked Paddy what he thought the horse was worth. Paddy is the great gentleman of Irish racing and he said that the question of price would not be his area at all. "Now that's something you will have to sort out with this man here," says Paddy. I have to say of the two of them that they were absolute gentlemen.

'Very often when people come to buy a horse from you there is a struggle to hammer out a deal, but that did not happen in this case. Christy asked me what I wanted, I told him and he said he would phone me back at 9 o'clock that night. Paddy had to go back to Doninga because there was a TV crew coming to do an item on Dawn Run. Christy phoned me at 9 o'clock to arrange for a vet to see the horse next day, and the deal was done.

'When you're selling a horse like this it's the custom to give somebody a small part of the price back for luck, but Christy only wanted a fiver. It was a pleasure doing business with the two of them. And I was glad to see the horse going on and winning a good few races for its new owner.'

Eddie Hayden originally bought Cloughtaney as a yearling in 1982 from the man who bred him, Sean Walsh. Sean, a brother of Eddie's wife Mary, runs Knockboy Stud at Gortnahoe, Thurles. Eddie put the horse in training himself. He originally had a permit to train his own horses. Then friends asked him to train their horses as well so he took out a licence. After Cloughtaney's first race which he did not win, the horse went on to win three bumpers in a row under Eddie

Hayden's tutelage, with Michael Holden in the saddle. The bumpers were at Clonmel (December 1985), Limerick (March 1986) and Fairyhouse (April 1986). It was the latter performance that convinced Christy Maye that he wanted to buy the horse.

Says Eddie, 'Cloughtaney was going from a small stable to a very big stable and I think it took him a while to settle in. He was a highly-strung horse. But then he started to win races. I thought the highlight of his career was when he won the Bookmakers Hurdle at Leopardstown. I was glad to see him win so many races for his new owner.' He's hoping that the settlement of a financial dispute with the banks over his land, a settlement that was hammered out in March 1995, will allow him to pay more attention to the several horses of his own that he still has in his stable.

Some time after Cloughtaney went to Paddy Mullins, the horse was entered for the £50,000 Sean Graham Hurdle at Leopardstown. Christy Maye can well remember going to Leopardstown with his wife to attend the race, on a miserable, rainy day, and looking at the huge trophy for the race, and thinking how nice it would be to win it. But at the same time he was being realistic, and was hoping that Cloughtaney might just run into a place. When Cloughtaney actually won the race in considerable style, Christy Maye was so full of euphoria in the parade ring that he says now he didn't even realise it was raining.

He pays tribute to the way Paddy Mullins trained Cloughtaney, sending him out to win eight times. In addition, when the horse didn't win, he was rarely out of the place money. He has particularly vivid memories of the time Cloughtaney won the Bishop Cleeve Hurdle at Cheltenham in 1988, easily beating some class horses, and winning from Beech Road and Mrs Muck. He also has great memories of the time Cloughtaney went to Aintree the following year for the Sandeman Hurdle. The race was won by Beech Road, but there was a photo for second and Peter Scudamore on Celtic Shot was convinced he had got up ahead of Cloughtaney to take second place. Cloughtaney's rider Tony Mullins was equally convinced that he was second. Scudamore came back into the stall for second place, while the Cloughtaney connections had to move into the stall for third. Then, much to the great joy of Christy Maye, it was announced that Cloughtaney had come second by a head. The occupancy of the stalls had to be quickly switched around. The result made a considerable difference financially – the prize money for second place was £7,800, while the prize for third was £3,700.

Ultimately, as happens with some horses, in the later stages of his career, Cloughtaney just seemed to lose interest. He is now living in retirement on Christy Maye's land at Mullingar, and is used for showjumping by his 14-year-old daughter Leanne. Paddy Mullins says, 'Cloughtaney was a good horse for us. Towards the end of his racing career, he got fed up with the game. That's my reading of it anyway. He just did not want to know. He came to the end of his usefulness and went home . . . '

* * *

The year that Cloughtaney came to the Mullins stable, 1986, was notable in that it also saw the debut of Grabel, who was to write her own special chapter into the history of the Mullins yard. On 14 August that year, at Tramore, Charlie Swan rode Grabel to victory in the Woodtown Maiden. Two weeks later Mags Lennon, soon to be the bride of Tony Mullins, rode Grabel to win the Rose of Tralee race at the Tralee Festival. Then, ridden by Peter Kavanagh, Grabel took the Juvenile Maiden Hurdle at Navan and ended the year in fine style by taking the Sean Graham Memorial Hurdle at the Leopardstown Christmas meeting. Grabel was to go on to do even better things. The total number of winners recorded for the Mullins stable in 1986 was 64. And among the good performers who contributed to that total during the year and who went on to become good money earners for the yard were Darkorjon, Derrymore Boy and Tradehimin.

The second part of the 1980s was significant for Paddy Mullins from a family point of view. His sons Willy and Tony both got married, both set up as trainers in their own right, and both continued to ride in races, as did their wives. Willy tied the knot in 1986 and began training just over a year later. Tony married his fiancée Mags in 1987 and continued as first jockey to his father, while setting up his own training operation. Tony had his first win as a trainer when his charge Clever Christian, ridden by the late David Parnell, won the prestigious Red Sunset Birdcatcher Nursery at Naas in October 1987. The horse was then sold to America for a handsome profit. Tony's wife rode winners on Innocent Choice during that same year, while Paddy's daughter Sandra also kept the name of the Mullins women up in lights when she won a bumper on Innocent Choice at Leopardstown.

Meanwhile, back at the home stable in Doninga, the year's tally of winners amounted to 62. Tony was to crown his first year as a trainer by notching up a valuable win in July 1988 by sending out Afford A King to take the Galway Plate in the hands of his Gowran neighbour Padge Gill. It was the last Galway Festival to be overseen by Paddy's brother Luke before his retirement as manager of Galway racecourse. So it was particularly appropriate that Luke's nephew should take the premier prize at the festival as he himself bowed out. This year, 1988, was indeed to prove a vintage year for the Mullins racing dynasty. Paddy's tally of winners was 83, making him champion trainer over jumps for the sixth year in a row. That same year Willy was the leading amateur rider while Tony was just pipped for the Jockey's Championship by Tommy Carmody.

As Paddy's sons got their own training careers under way, he let them do their own thing, without interfering, although always glad to help out in an emergency. Says Willy, 'When I started my father let me get on with it, never interfered and never told me what I should be doing or should not be doing. He reckoned I had seen enough and it was time now for me to go ahead and do it and make my own mistakes. It's probably the best way. You start off a lot more slowly but you appreciate your lessons much more.' Willy had his first winner as a trainer in February 1988 when his charge Silver Batchelor won a bumper at Thurles. Like his father before him on his first win as a trainer, Willy himself rode Silver Batchelor to victory.

At the Cheltenham Festival in 1988, Paddy Mullins had no fewer than three sons riding in the Champion Hurdle, adding yet another item to the record books. Willy rode Grabel, Tony was on Cloughtaney while Tom partnered Tradehimin. The brothers had no success, although Cloughtaney put in a good performance, staying with the leaders until three out when he weakened. Few racegoers on the day knew of the drama behind the scenes before the race. Sandra was driving her brothers to the racecourse from the holiday cottage complex where they had all been staying, when they became caught up in the traffic jam to end all traffic jams. Tony was also to ride Redundant Pal in the first race of the day. The brothers thought they had left plenty of time to get to the racecourse, but when the traffic refused to move, they almost began to panic. The idea of having to face their father after missing out on three rides in the Champion Hurdle did not bear thinking about. The three were thinking of hitching rides on police motor bikes when Sandra managed to get off the main road, and, driving furiously along back roads, found a way into the racecourse complex just in time. It was one race – this time against time itself – that she was really glad to win.

During that same year Sandra had another stint of skilful driving but this time it was on Whassat, whom she steered to victory in the Pretty Polly Hosiery ladies' race at Killarney on 14 July. Sandra has a particular memory of this event, for some free samples of tights were given to herself and to her mother and, obviously by some oversight, to Paddy as well. Sandra won again with the same horse in an amateur handicap at Leopardstown on 1 August, beating into second place Tigh an Cheoil, ridden by Norman Williamson, now one of the leading National Hunt jockeys. Says Sandra, 'Norman got a terrible ribbing from people at his own yard, O'Grady's, over being beaten by a married woman, but he was not long about evening up the score when he won on our next encounter on a racecourse!' The year 1989 saw some of the stars of the Mullins stable doing well, including Redundant Pal and The Gooser. The stable recorded a total of 58 winners for the year.

CHAPTER 15

In the Blood

Paddy Mullins was startled to hear his name called out over the public address system. It was 6 April 1990, and he was attending the annual trainers' lunch given by Ivan Straker at Aintree during the week of the Grand National. Straker, a key figure in race sponsorship, hosts a lunch every year that has now become one of the highlights of the social scene for trainers from both Ireland and the UK. Paddy was enjoying the lunch, as he did not have a runner in the immediate aftermath, and he was startled by the message asking him to go to the weigh room. He says, 'I was concerned – I said to myself, "What's up now?" When he got to the weigh room, the trainer Martin Pipe and the jockey Peter Scudamore were waiting to talk to him. He had never met either of them before. Pipe apologised for taking Paddy away from the lunch and went on to explain why he needed a quiet word. Scudamore was about to ride Sayparee in a hurdle race for the first time. The horse was quite new to the Pipe stable but had been bred by Paddy and had also been trained by him before being sold to England. So clearly Paddy was the man who knew Sayparee probably better than anybody else and Martin Pipe wanted to find out what advice the Goresbridge trainer might have for Scudamore.

Says Paddy, 'I advised Scudamore to hold him up and really hold him up, and even when you think you should go, don't go.' Paddy watched the race with considerable interest, hoping that his advice would work out for Scudamore and hoping that he hadn't scuppered the jockey's chances. Scu did exactly as Paddy had told him. Sayparee travelled well throughout the race, but Scudamore did not urge him into a real burst of speed until the final 100 yards. He won by a length. Paddy's advice had worked out and the Doninga man allowed himself a quiet sigh of relief.

Paddy recalls, 'Scudamore just lay out at the back of the field, and appeared to make absolutely no effort early on, just as I had advised. He carried out the instructions to the letter, and you would think this fellow is not trying, if you didn't know the strategy. And then somewhere in the last furlong he just loosed the reins and said "go" and he just demolished them.' It was Scudamore's only winner at the Aintree meeting that year, and he was particularly pleased with it. In his book, *The Autobiography of a Champion*, Scudamore pays tribute to Paddy's help. Scudamore remarks, 'This victory I put down to the advice of Sayparee's breeder, the great Irish trainer Paddy Mullins, who told me to hold the horse up for as long as possible.'

Paddy comments, 'This encounter with Martin Pipe showed me what a perfectionist he is. He did not know me well enough to phone me but he knew I was at the meeting and had me called over the tannoy and then asked my advice. It was an exceptional thing to happen. In my experience quite a few other trainers and jockeys in similar circumstances would have the belief they know more than this fool who had the horse previously. There is a lot of pride involved in this business and some trainers don't want to appear to need advice from somebody else. Even if you tried to tell some of them something, they don't want to be told. Martin Pipe was being very professional.'

Sayparee was out of a mare, Parijatak that Paddy had at Doninga – and indeed still has, although she is at an advanced age. She grazes in a lush paddock behind the house. He is hoping he might have another foal out of her, but even if he does not, he is a little sentimental about the animal and is prepared to let her laze away her days in peace. Parijatak belonged to a wealthy Indian businessman who was introduced to Paddy by Johnny Roe, the veteran jockey who used to ride for him in the old days. Johnny is an old pal of Paddy's, and has been involved in the racing business in various exotic parts of the world, from India to Hong Kong. Johnny, who presently lives in Macao, is always glad to refer foreign owners to Paddy, and an Indian millionaire, a Mr Goculdas, was one of these. Johnny used to ride in India for Mr Goculdas, who had a brood mare and a yearling at a stud in England. Through Johnny's influence, the mare and the yearling were sent to the Mullins yard in the 1970s. The yearling was Parijatak. The owner and his wife came to Doninga a couple of times, and once explained to Paddy that, translated, 'parijatak' means a small Indian flower.

Parijatak was run a couple of times, but then Mr Goculdas, who made his fortune from the bottled gas business, decided he wanted to get out of having horses in Ireland, and he let Paddy have Parijatak, along with her dam, quite cheaply. Parijatak won quite a few races – her first win was in a bumper at Mallow in August 1975, the Lee Maiden Hurdle, with Paddy's son Willy riding. Says Paddy, 'She was from a really top family of the Aga Khan's – her ancestry went back to the dam of Nasrullah. We bred Sayparee from her, who was born in 1985. Sayparee was by a stallion, Saher. I liked his pedigree. He was by Great Nephew, the sire of Shergar, and we bred a few by him. I foolishly thought that in this case I might breed a Shergar! Another reason for using Saher was that he was on our doorstep – at Burgage Stud down the road. The stud is owned by the Connolly family and they rented it to a Frenchman, Jacques Perrot, who also had a couple of horses with me. We didn't win much with Sayparee but then he just blossomed at this particular stage and won and Jonjo O'Neill wanted him for a client. So we did a deal and Jonjo bought him. Sayparee must have been only four when we sold him. The horse later went to Martin Pipe.'

Breeding horses has always been an interest of Paddy's although he feels he hasn't bred anything of earth-shattering significance. He always has some brood mares at his place in

Doninga. He never kept a stallion because it would be too time-consuming. He regrets sometimes that he did not have a stallion at the stable – if only for the tax breaks involved. Parijatak would be the brood mare he has had for the longest number of years, even though she had to be handled carefully. He says, 'She wasn't a great breeder. You had to handle her well. If she got too fat she would never go in foal. Her first foal was by Lock Diamond. Pariglit we called him. He was a brilliant horse. Her really good horse was Pargan, by Tarqogan. I knew there was a lot of speed in Tarqogan. I remember seeing him win as a two-year-old in the Phoenix Park one day and he literally ran away from a big field of two-year-olds. Pargan I counted the best that Parijatak produced. Pargan won the Players Amateur race at Galway with Willy riding him. He was a small horse, too. He'd have won doing handstands, with 12st 7lb on his back. Later he broke down and was finally put down.

'I have other brood mares also, and would try to have them in foal every year, if possible. I have three barren mares this year (1995). Brood mares take more looking after than other horses. We have not a stud as such, we have a training stable, and the stables in the winter are full of racehorses and therefore I don't want brood mares cluttering up too much space.'

Paddy Mullins has made a life-long study of breeding and is of the opinion that many top equine families have suffered from the introduction of too much staying power, and have become slow. 'From my studies breeders tend to go for Derby winners and Gold Cup winners and after the introduction of a couple of these sires, the speed is gone. It happens all the time. I'm told the Aga Khan's advice on breeding was to keep introducing speed, and more speed, if you want to keep up a family, and I would agree with that. Often people can't afford these top speed sires, the ones who are going to keep the pedigree right – I'm talking primarily of the Flat. But even in jumping if you lose the speed you're gone as well.'

As a by-product of his interest in breeding, Paddy has been fascinated by pedigree, and has an incredible memory when it comes to the ancestry of individual horses. His son Tony says,

'It was unbelievable the way he would follow up a horse's pedigree or ancestry. I remember a horse coming to the stable one time. There was a string of noughts behind him – he had come nowhere in a long time. At this stage I did not realise that the other trainer who had him before knew he was a good horse and was letting him develop. And this trainer had done an expert job. Not knowing the background, I thought this looks desperate. And I went into the dining room and my father had all these books out and he says "I remember that one in 1928" – referring to one of the horse's ancestors, and this was 60 years on.

'He believed it was in the pedigree and that it could come back again. And it did. It's an awful pity that he did not do some of those statistical records, because he was brilliant at determining why a family had gone bad, and how the wrong blood had come in. He is the best I ever met at it. He goes through those horses, and can say why a particular stallion might have been bad for that particular family and so forth. He is still deeply involved in breeding himself. If somebody wins a bumper in Ballinrobe by ten lengths, he's driving home as hard as he can to get to the stud books to know why this horse won so well. He might not be home until one o'clock in the morning and everyone else would be worn out but he would be straight in to the dining room where he has all these stud books and he would pick out some horse from 40 years ago that was a good horse and he would figure that's why the family is good. He would go through all those things. It wasn't that he felt it a duty – he just loved doing it.'

Paddy Mullins's passion for the study of pedigrees rubbed off on one of the lads who used to work at the stable – with impressive results. As a youngster, Jim Murphy would bombard the trainer with questions about the role of breeding in determining a horse's character and ability. Jim, who grew up near the Mullins yard, was to become chief travelling lad at Doninga, and was with Dawn Run on almost all of her expeditions abroad and, of course, was there when the mare was killed. He is now a very successful bloodstock dealer, and has his own stud farm, the Red Pender stud, at Castlekelly, near Goresbridge. Jim acknowledges that it was from Paddy Mullins that he first gained the knowledge that enabled him later to set up in business on his own.

As with many of the people who have worked at Doninga, there is a family connection going back a couple of generations. Jim's father, Nicholas 'Nicksie' Murphy worked for a while for Paddy Mullins's father on the farm at Doninga House, and also did some riding out. From the time he started going to school, Jim Murphy was interested in the horses at the Mullins yard, and he would go there after school to look at the horses, and even do a few chores because he enjoyed the work. He recalls, 'I remember feeding Hurry Harriet and Rising Gull when I was going to school, aged 9 or 10. They used to be in a field called the Long Meadow. We lived in one of the houses at the Slate Range – that's a row of four houses right beside the road on the way to Goresbridge. Then we moved up to Doninga, opposite the yard. My father is still living there. Paddy Mullins was brilliant to explain pedigrees to a youngster. You would be asking so many stupid questions, but he was always glad to talk. I would ask him loads of questions as a youngster about a horse's background, how he breeds horses, how come one horse is nice and another lad is not. That's the way I learned the basis of the work I do now.

'My first job after leaving school was in Mullins's. I didn't really think of anything else. But I did not go into it with big ideas of being a jockey or anything like that. I was about 16. I was a lad. A lad would muck out and ride out and brush over horses and do whatever other jobs might need to be done. I was wicked slow to learn how to ride a horse. They had ponies there in the beginning and I did a bit of learning on the ponies. The sons had ponies. Many youngsters around here would have experimented on the ponies. I used to ride out the horses, and rode in about 80 races. I won one race – which shows that miracles can happen. The horse was Dudie, and I won in the colours of Paddy's daughter Sandra. I left Doninga a few years ago and work on my own now. I buy foals and sell them as yearlings. If the markets are good you're okay and if they are bad, well . . . I breed as well – I've a couple of brood mares. Jim Prendergast used to own this place where I am now. He was a great card player, and they used to call him the Red Pender and I just put it down as the name of the stud. As regards the knowledge, it all goes back to the great trainer, Paddy Mullins.'

Paddy Mullins pays tribute to the achievements of Jim Murphy. 'Jim is a very successful bloodstock man. I knew that when he was a lad here working that he was very intelligent. Whatever knowledge he picked up remained with him. He started off by buying a brood mare and he would sell a foal and buy another, leading to where he is now, owning his own stud farm. He is highly successful at buying and selling. If I wanted a reference to a horse he would be one of the first fellows I would ask. Jim Murphy can go to the sales and buy yearlings or foals, bring them home and sell them, and is as well known in Doncaster and Newmarket as the biggest agent at the present time. He would give £40,000 or £50,000 for a foal. He is one of the success stories of this establishment.'

* * *

Tom O'Leary could have been forgiven for changing his mind and deciding not to buy The Gooser. For the very first time the Dublin businessman encountered the horse, at the Ballsbridge Sales, the animal suddenly kicked out and caught Tom full on the chin, sending him flying with the force of the impact. The incident happened in a passageway, before the horse entered the ring. Tom O'Leary was lucky to avoid being killed. He was also fortunate that his jaw was not broken. But he was bleeding from the ears, suffered some painful injuries to the mouth, and was to lose some teeth. He was in the company of Paddy Mullins's son Tony at the time, and Tony and others rushed to help him, but he was able to continue with the business of the sales.

Tom's schoolboy son Jarlath was horrified to witness his father being floored by the horse, and pleaded with his father,

191

as the animal came into the ring, 'Daddy, don't buy him, he'll kill you.' But Tom O'Leary, a businessman who ran a successful crane hire concern, reassured his son that all would be well, and went ahead and purchased The Gooser for 8,000 guineas. The horse was a present for Tom's wife Margaret who had been a follower of racing ever since her early childhood in Bunclody, Co. Wexford. Her father had brought her to the races at the age of four, and she had never lost her interest in the sport of kings. The Gooser was sent to Paddy Mullins for training and was to give Tom and Margaret O'Leary great enjoyment and excitement, and many wins, including the Galway Plate in 1992. And despite The Gooser's violent first encounter with Tom O'Leary, Paddy Mullins found him one of the most docile horses one could encounter. Paddy is still a little mystified as to why the horse lashed out that day. He says, 'It was an unusual thing to happen. Unaccountably, the horse let fly. He was an unbroken four-year-old at the time. But he turned out to be the quietest horse.'

The involvement of Tom and Margaret O'Leary in the ownership of horses went back to 1982. Tom O'Leary had a friend who worked in the office of the Director of Public Prosecutions, and who had a horse. For just a few hundred pounds, Tom bought a half share in the horse, Legal Buck, as a present for his wife. The horse was sent for training to Ted Walsh, and it was also envisaged that Ted would ride him in races. But tragedy struck as the horse was being exercised on the gallops. He met with an accident and was killed, before he ever had a chance to take part in a race. That was the bad news. The good news was that Margaret, through beginner's luck, had decided to insure the horse for £5,000. With the aid of the insurance pay-out, Tom O'Leary bought another horse, Noir Shoon, and he was sent for training to Paddy Mullins. Noir Shoon went on to win a number of races, but was injured and had to be put down. Then came the transaction to buy The Gooser, in June 1986.

The Gooser was to prove one of the more successful horses in the Paddy Mullins stable during the late 1980s and early

192

1990s. The Gooser won quite a few races, one of the more valuable being the Kerry National in Listowel in 1990. Margaret O'Leary, and indeed Paddy Mullins himself, will always remember when the horse went on to win the Galway Plate in 1992. Paddy had been looking for a suitable jockey to ride The Gooser in the race, but had run into some problems. He had approached three leading Irish jockeys, but nobody was free to take the ride. Then Adrian Maguire phoned up to see if he could partner The Gooser and Paddy did not have to think twice about it. Maguire who, the following year, was to go on to become No. 1 rider at 'The Duke' Nicholson's stables at Jackdaws Castle in the English Midlands, got a dream of a ride from The Gooser. Maguire could not believe how easily he was travelling as The Gooser flew up in the hill in the closing stages of the race to beat another Mullins horse, Baptismal Fire into second place. For Paddy Mullins it was a very satisfying result, to have two of his charges taking first and second place in the Galway Plate. Baptismal Fire was owned by one of Paddy's long-term clients, solicitor Fergus Taaffe, and the horse was ridden on the day by Jason Titley. Jason had perfected his riding skills while a lad at the Mullins yard, and in 1995 he won fame by riding Royal Athlete to victory in the Aintree Grand National. Third behind The Gooser in the Galway Plate was Four Trix, ridden by Richard Dunwoody.

There was a champagne reception after the Galway Plate victory, but the real celebration was a couple of weeks later when the O'Learys held a big open-air lunch in the garden of their secluded home at Dalkey, Co. Dublin. Paddy and Maureen Mullins were there. Says Margaret, 'Paddy enjoyed the lunch enormously. By then he had got to know us and was at ease with us. When he gets to know you, and can relax in your company, he's great fun, and a great story teller. But when we knew him first, we'd ask him how The Gooser was, and we'd get a one-word reply, "Fine". Now, I think of him like a father. He's a marvellous trainer, and the most honest man you could meet.'

Margaret O'Leary is glad that her husband lived to see the

Galway Plate victory. Just three months later, he was dead. Tom O'Leary collapsed from a heart attack in a Dublin pub, The Stillorgan Orchard. It's a popular rendezvous for racegoers and Tom had gone there with some friends, including Willy Mullins, after attending a Leopardstown race meeting. The Gooser had been entered for the Thyestes Chase at Gowran Park just a couple of weeks later and Margaret O'Leary decided to leave the horse in the race, as she figured that's what her late husband would have wanted.

The Gooser was Paddy's entry in the Aintree Grand National in 1993, the year the race was aborted due to the false start. Says Margaret O'Leary, 'Paddy decided that The Gooser could have a go at the Grand National. I've always trusted his judgment totally – he has superb judgment when it comes to placing horses in races. The Gooser was in fine form on the day and I think he could have run into a place had the race not been called off.' She added that, typically, Paddy did not give any indication as to what his reaction was when the race was cancelled. The Gooser has since retired. He has been a good servant and Margaret O'Leary plans to let him live out his days at his ease. In Paddy Mullins's words, 'The Gooser is now a pensioner.' Margaret has two other horses in training in Doninga, Gambolling Doc and Gale Toi, both of whom have won races. She has also put another horse into training with Willy Mullins, the oddly-named Bobbit Back On.

* * *

During the 1990s Johnny Roe sent Paddy a client who proceeded to put a Flat horse in training at Doninga. The client was unusual in that Paddy never met him, or spoke to him – even on the phone. All communications were via the fax machine. The client was a Hong Kong millionaire businessman called P. Loo. Paddy never found out what the 'P' stood for. Johnny Roe had arranged for an agent to buy a yearling for Mr Loo and the animal was sent to Doninga. He was named Bernard's Toy, and he was a very slow developer. Paddy thought at first he would never win a race but then, as sometimes happens, the horse began to show much improvement. Finally Bernard's Toy won a Flat race at Galway on 7 September 1994, which qualified him to go and compete in certain races in Hong Kong. Mr Loo was over the moon and there was a flurry of ecstatic faxes to Doninga. Arrangements were made immediately to put Bernard's Toy into quarantine at Newmarket before being sent on to Hong Kong. Paddy has heard no more of Bernard's Toy – nor of his mysterious owner, Mr P. Loo . . .

CHAPTER 16

The Biggest Prize in the World

It was the mother of all parties. It went on all night and the champagne flowed like water. And during the hooley in Kentucky, USA, the normally reticent Paddy Mullins even broke into song. To the surprise and to the delight of those present, the trainer treated his audience to an old Irish ballad, *The Rose of Mooncoin*. He got a standing ovation. Paddy had good reason to celebrate – one of his horses had just taken the biggest prize ever in the history of jump racing. Despite a long, gruelling, difficult trip from Ireland, Grabel had won the $750,000 Dueling Grounds International Hurdle, and had put herself into the record books by doing so. Paddy was delighted that a mare he had trained had taken the first prize of $300,000. No doubt he was also delighted that his son Tony was in the saddle for the spectacular win. But Paddy had an additional reason to be pleased – his wife Maureen had a half share in Grabel, the man with the other half share being Wexford-born businessman Paddy Kehoe.

Paddy Kehoe is a fast-talking, quick-thinking, high-rolling gambler who generally has an entourage of pals with him when he hits a racecourse. A former bookmaker who has been involved in owning horses since the early 1980s, he seldom seems to smile – it's as if the business of betting and gambling and studying form is too serious to allow levity. The highlight of his life-long connection with the racing game was when Grabel won the big prize at Bowling Green, Kentucky on

22 April 1990. Paddy, who runs a suspended ceiling business from his base in Dublin could have jumped up and hit one of his own suspended ceilings he was so delighted over the win. He says proudly, 'There is only one horse won more money than Grabel in National Hunt racing, and that was Desert Orchid. Grabel won £435,000 in her career. I think she won on nearly every track she went on, with six different jockeys, on the Flat, over hurdles, any distance, any ground, it didn't make any difference to her.

'I would safely say her win in Kentucky was the greatest training feat of all time. Grabel travelled out to New York on a Tuesday. She was in quarantine from Tuesday until Saturday, walking around this little 20 feet by 20 feet area. Then she travelled 18 hours by road down to Kentucky on the Saturday. She only had a chance to jump a few hurdles and she went out and she beat the best horses in the world. And there wasn't a word about it. Very little coverage in the media. Paddy Mullins turned around to me when it was over and said, "You'll never see the likes of this again." Probably the only mistake we ever made is that after she won in America, and towards the end of her career, we turned down an offer from a syndicate of £210,000 for her.'

It was Paddy Mullins who, quite by chance, spotted Grabel for sale during a visit to England in the early 1980s. He had been asked to take part in a panel to judge the champion horse at Doncaster Sales. Paddy recalls, 'They always bring an Irish trainer over to make a panel of two or three trainers who pick out the champion at the sale, which is a National Hunt sale for store, or young, horses. This particular year I was asked to go over and I had no other business in Doncaster. The judging had taken place on a Sunday and I was at a loose end the following day before returning home. So to pass the time I had a look at the horses in the ring, spotted this particular mare and liked her. She was not even among the horses that were being judged – she was not in that class, and was too young anyway. This one was only two and they were mostly four-year-olds who were being judged. I liked what I saw as she walked around the ring.

'The first thing that attracted her to me was that I had trained her grandmother. The name of the grandmother, Slap Up, was in the catalogue. Slap Up had belonged to the Vigors family who ran Burgage Stud just a few miles from Doninga and they had also bred her. Slap Up belonged to an old family that Terence Vigors's father A. C. Vigors had when he lived in Tipperary, in what is now Coolmore Stud, before moving to Burgage Stud. The Vigors ran a very successful stud operation – they had Sovereign Path, a top stallion of his time and Terence had been joint Master with my father in the Mount Loftus Harriers.

'From previous experience I knew that buying an animal without having a really good look at her would be very unwise. So I didn't bid and she went out of the ring unsold at 900 guineas. I felt that 1,000 guineas would have bought her but I daren't bid for her until I had a good look at her outside. I looked at her very carefully and decided that maybe she could be bought. I contacted Dick Morgan, a bloodstock agent who is a very good judge of a horse. He had an office in Doncaster as well as in Dublin. I asked him if he could go and buy her for me, which he did. I think that she cost 1,000 guineas. I was thrilled to get her for that money. I suppose only she was going so cheaply I would not have bothered. I took her home and broke her and gave her a couple of runs in the autumn and she showed a little promise. She also showed some promise as a three-year-old. She won the first time out at Tramore, with Charlie Swan riding her. Charlie was apprenticed to Kevin Prendergast at the time. Tony later took over. She had won races by the time that Paddy Kehoe became involved in her.'

There was, as often happens in deals to do with Irish racehorses, a go-between involved when Paddy Kehoe was buying into Grabel in 1988. A friend of his, who was also friendly with Paddy's son Willy, knew that Kehoe wanted to acquire a decent horse, and this man, a keen observer of the racing scene and an excellent judge of a horse, suggested Grabel. Paddy Kehoe became convinced he should invest in

Grabel because it was the second time within a couple of weeks that the mare had been recommended to him. Says Kehoe, 'Quite independently a friend of mine, Jack Quinn, who used to play for Meath, had advised me to buy Grabel – he saw her winning at Fairyhouse as a three-year-old. He thought she had great potential. It was a strange coincidence that Jack Quinn had mentioned it to me and then my contact came on the phone a couple of weeks later to make a similar recommendation. I was introduced to Mr and Mrs Mullins. I would have bought Grabel outright, but Mrs Mullins said she wanted to keep a half share.'

Paddy Mullins recalls how the go-between came to him and said that if they wanted to sell Grabel, Paddy Kehoe would buy. 'We didn't want to sell but we agreed to sell a half share, and the mare ran in Paddy Kehoe's name. Grabel began showing promise from an early stage and she was always able to surprise me. She had beautiful action and racing took very little out of her. She was one of the most successful mares we had.'

Paddy Kehoe was no stranger to involvement in racehorses – some of them successful. Sitting in a Dublin pub, a pint in front of him, Paddy Kehoe talks about his horses in his usual staccato, rapid-fire style. 'First horse I ever owned was a horse called Gambler's Wish. He was trained by Henry Cleary and won a point-to-point in Shillelagh one day. That was my first winner, about 1986 or 1987. Next horse I owned was trained by John McAuley in the north, a fairly decent horse. A novice 'chaser. He never won a race. I had a quarter share in Antarctic Bay that won the Sun Alliance Chase at Cheltenham in 1985. That was the first decent horse I was involved in. Trained by Pat Hughes. Then I had a third share in Abbey Glen which was beaten in a photo finish in the Arkle Chase in Cheltenham, a few years ago. He was a real good horse. He broke down.'

Grabel was the best horse Paddy Kehoe was involved in. He says, 'Grabel was like a bank – a licence to print money. No doubt about it. She used to win races by 20 lengths. Grabel was carrying 12 stone on her back for much of her career – and that's when you know you have a good one – when she is carrying that kind of weight. She won 24 races for us – 11 times in Punchestown – was never beaten in Punchestown. She won the Guinness Four-Year-Old Championship in Punchestown the first year, and beat Aldino and Classical Charm in that race, and Classical Charm was beaten in a photo finish in the Champion Hurdle the following year. Aldino was favourite for the Triumph Hurdle that year. Then Grabel won three bookmakers' hurdles at Punchestown, three years on the trot. She won the first Sean Graham £50,000 race at Leopardstown and she won three bookmakers' hurdles at Leopardstown. She won the big hurdle race in Down Royal three years on the trot. She won a couple of Flat races in Gowran Park and Dundalk.

'She was never beaten in a photo finish. She won three times at Punchestown by short heads. And she won twice at Leopardstown by short heads. She was always able to stick her neck out. Tony was brilliant on her. Only for him I don't think she would have won any of those photo finishes. I always liked Tony Mullins. When Tony was riding for you, when he went off to the front he always got a good run, and nearly always won. Nowadays you have jockeys coming from behind and they don't know what they're at. Tony always gave you a good run. He often had races won from the start. Finally Grabel broke down – wear and tear. She had to be racing all the time. If she was left off, she went back. She loved racing.'

In 1990 came the invitation to the race that was to be the highlight of Grabel's career – the richest jump race ever run, the Dueling Grounds International Hurdle. Paddy Mullins had been interested in the race from the time he first heard about it. So when Cheltenham racecourse manager Edward Gillespie phoned on behalf of the Kentucky organisers to offer a place to Grabel, Paddy immediately said 'yes'. The race was to be held at a new racecourse in Bowling Green, Kentucky, close by a site where Southern gentlemen like Sam Houston and Andrew Jackson settled differences with pistols. The racecourse had been built right beside the border with Tennessee, a non-betting state, and was only 15 miles from Nashville, Tennessee. The idea was that people from Tennessee could go to the racecourse and gamble. (Ironically, while Kentucky allowed betting, it had severe restrictions on alcohol sales, which did not apply across the border in Tennessee. As one Irishman who attended the big race remarked, 'You could lose your shirt betting on one side of the state line, and get plastered drunk on the other side, but you couldn't do both at the same time.')

About 20,000 people turned out for the opening of the racecourse – and to see the running of the Dueling Grounds International Hurdle. While Tony Mullins had been quite confident setting out from Ireland, his hopes had faded considerably because of difficulties that arose during the long journey. He recalls, 'There had been terrible pressure. The quarantine went wrong. The mare had done nothing for a full week and we thought it was pointless taking part. We fancied her before we left but then we get there and the mare has been 18 hours in a box, has not been trotted for a week and we thought we did not have a hope. Being short of the work we thought she would go to the second last and just fade out.' During the extremely difficult journey from Ireland, Grabel was under the constant care of Valerie Crean, from Nurney, Co. Carlow, travelling head girl at the time with the Mullins stable. While the mare was in quarantine, Valerie was not allowed to ride her out. The only exercise permitted was long walks. For her role in bringing Grabel safely through that difficult, marathon journey, Valerie was later to be the inaugural winner of the Bisquit Cognac-*Irish Independent* Racing Award.

Apart from the rigours of a difficult journey and the lack of work, there was another reason not to run Grabel – the condition of the track. Paddy Mullins was not impressed at all, and began to realise now why some American horses had been withdrawn. When he walked the course he found that the track was in very poor shape. Says the trainer, 'The track was supposed to be ready and the rains came during the winter and then it dried out and the track had sunk here and there and become bare in patches. I should have suspected when the American horses started pulling out of the race. But I did not realise what it was like until I walked it and by then the die was cast. If we didn't run we were not going to get the $10,000 subsidy for bringing Grabel out.' Paddy Mullins considered withdrawing Grabel from the race but after a consultation with Paddy Kehoe, it was ultimately decided to go ahead. Says Paddy Kehoe, 'I left the decision to Paddy Mullins. I said I would go along with whatever he decided. It was a very long way to go and then withdraw.'

As the race got under way, Paddy Kehoe was watching from the stewards' box – the stands had not yet been completed. A fanatical Wexford GAA fan, he had earlier listened to the Wexford *v* Kilkenny hurling match commentary by telephone. He was disappointed when Wexford were beaten but Tony Mullins cheered him up by saying, 'It's okay, nothing to worry about – we'll still do it for Kilkenny!'

Grabel, on the day, seemed to relish the hard going that other horses in the race were to find exhausting. The only mare in a field of nine, Grabel took command before the 11th of the 12 fences in the two and three quarter mile race and powered on to win by two and a quarter lengths from the American horse Uptown Swell. Another American horse Polar Pleasure came in third, followed by Peer Prince (US), Summer Colony (US), Nomadic Way (UK) and Valrodian (New Zealand). Cheltenham winner Regal Ambition (UK) and Collins (France) were both pulled up. Regal Ambition had led until Grabel took up the running and was subsequently found to have broken down. Nomadic Way, ridden by Richard Dunwoody, had been favourite. Grabel was recording the 23rd success of her career on the Flat and over jumps. It was her sixth consecutive win, and it's reckoned she was the first Irish-trained National Hunt winner in America. Paddy Kehoe was asked by a reporter, 'When did you first realise you were going to win the race?' The Wexford man quipped, 'Three weeks ago!'

Says Paddy Mullins, 'When Grabel won, my reaction was disbelief, coupled with delight. I could not believe it that she could beat the eight horses in the race. I didn't have a bet on that day.' Paddy Kehoe had backed Grabel, as he thought, but when he went to collect his winnings he found that his bet had been recorded, not for Grabel, but for another horse in a different race. There had been an announcement over the loudspeaker earlier in the day warning punters that they would have to get their bets on straight away. Kehoe went immediately to put on his money, but he was betting on the wrong race, and later kicked up an enormous fuss. Recalls Tony Mullins with a grin, 'The roars of Paddy when he found they were not going to pay him were something else.'

Paddy Kehoe was paid his money in the end – about $30,000. He says the fact that he was ultimately paid was an indication that the mistake was not on his part, but on the part of the Tote authorities. 'The Tote staff backed me up,' said Kehoe. 'Only for that I would not have been paid. Grabel was returned at 5–1, but according to the form she could have been favourite. It certainly wasn't my biggest ever gamble, but as regards prize money, it was my biggest win.' The messages of congratulation poured into Doninga after the big win, which had helped to give Grabel the record in prize winnings for an Irish National Hunt horse. Vincent O'Brien and his wife Jacqueline, no strangers themselves to big money wins, sent a fax, 'Many congratulations on Grabel's wonderful win. We were thrilled for you all.'

Several years on, Paddy Kehoe gets excited just by the thought of the opposition that Grabel trounced on that sunny day in Kentucky. 'Just look at some of the other horses in the race. Regal Ambition was in it – and Regal Ambition won the Sun Alliance hurdle by 25 lengths. Nomadic Way was in it – and Nomadic Way was beaten in two photo finishes in the Champion Hurdle, as well as winning two Irish Champion Hurdles and the Stayers Hurdle in Cheltenham the following year. There was a horse in it that was tailed off, Valrodian, and he came over to Leopardstown the following year and won the Arkle Chase. No matter what horse ever finished within the same field as Grabel, we always won. We were unlucky in Cheltenham the same year. Grabel was a 6/1 chance for the Champion Hurdle of 1990 when she was withdrawn four days before the race due to sinus. The ground was ideal for her and she would have hacked up, as was proved afterwards. Nomadic Way was only beaten by a head.'

On the day of the big win, the Governor of Kentucky presented the trophy, and the celebrations began in the open air. As it was a 'dry' county, Paddy Kehoe had sent a 'gofer' off in a big Cherokee jeep to buy booze in the next state, Tennessee, and he came back with $1,500 worth of drink for the hooley, packed into a laundry basket that had been borrowed from the Irish party's hotel. Kehoe laid in the booze by the winner's enclosure before the race, so confident was he of a good result. Recalls Kehoe, 'Everybody joined in the celebrations. Richard Dunwoody, Martin Pipe, Steve Smith-Eccles were all there. Everybody connected with the race was there. There were at least 25 in the party over from Ireland. We were doling out the booze, and then we went back into the complex and the people who ran the race had a room upstairs and I never saw as much drink in one room in all my life. I suppose there was 100 people there. I remember about 10 p.m. the man who owned the place came in and there was not a drink left for him.

'The police made sure we got back to our hotel safely – the Holiday Inn. We had a great session back in the hotel. We took over two suites of rooms upstairs. There were pressmen there from all over America. Paddy Mullins sang *The Rose of Mooncoin*. I couldn't believe it.' The Irish contingent was joined by friends from New York, Chicago and Florida. John Byrne, a Gaelic games reporter with the *Irish Echo* who had left Doninga more than 50 years before to emigrate to America, made his way from New York to Kentucky to shake the hand of his old neighbour and childhood friend, Paddy Mullins.

Paddy Kehoe wasn't long in losing a sizeable slice of the money he won in Kentucky when Grabel ran at Ascot after her return to Europe. He had £25,000 on Grabel, and he wasn't the only punter to bet heavily on the mare. 'I'd say the biggest gamble ever on a horse was on Grabel that year at Ascot. Pat Eddery rode her in the Queen Alexandra Stakes. She was backed from 3/1 down to 2/5. There was over £1 million in bets on her – £120,000 to win £80,000; £140,000 to win £100,000.

There were big bets like that on her. She was pulled up.' Still, he says he can't complain about his gambles on the mare. 'I won a lot of money on Grabel, gambling. I won £100,000 on her one Christmas gambling. The year she won the Sean Graham Hurdle, I had £9,000 on her at ten to one, but overall at the same meeting I lost £15,000.'

Has he come out ahead? 'Nobody wins. I'm losing. You can't win. You need to have the patience to wait and then you can't get on. I'm the unluckiest gambler in the world – and that's a fact. I had a very good Cheltenham in 1994 – I won £60,000. That's the last time I won. My horse with Paddy Mullins, Near Gale, was beaten twice in early 1995. I had £25,000 on her one day and £20,000 on her another day. She was beaten in two photo finishes. It takes a long time to recover from those kind of losses. It's heartbreaking.'

Grabel broke down in the end, and Paddy Mullins has a strong suspicion that the track on which she won her biggest prize was to blame. 'I'm sure that her breakdown, although it didn't happen on the day, was caused by the track on which she won the Kentucky race,' he says. Grabel was sold for a very good price as a brood mare, and is in a stud near Mullingar run by Mr Michael Kiernan. She has had a colt by Strong Gale and a filly by Montelimar. So how would Paddy Mullins rate Grabel? 'She was not in the same league as Dawn Run, but she was still a brilliant race mare. She would never carry the weights that Dawn Run could carry, but she was all heart.' Ironically, although Dawn Run was a better mare and achieved far more fame than Grabel, in terms of prize money it was Grabel who was the easy winner.

In 1992 Paddy Kehoe was in the news when it emerged he was one of the masterminds behind a syndicate formed to buy up a huge range of lottery tickets with a view to winning the Irish Lotto. The Lotto bosses did not take kindly to the operation and there was much controversy surrounding the affair. Paddy's gamble on the Lotto met with mixed fortunes. While the syndicate did come up with a winning number, unfortunately for the members there were two other winning tickets as well. The Lotto jackpot of £1.75 million had to be divided three ways, with the syndicate getting just over £568,000 – a third of the sum the members had hoped for. Says Paddy Kehoe, 'You could not be happy really with the result because of the three-way split. I made maybe £20,000 or £25,000. I'd have made £150,000 if we had won on our own.' As regards Grabel, he remarked, 'A few of us went down to see the mare one night a while ago. We got as far as the local pub – and never got any further.'

* * *

Back in the 1980s Paddy acquired a new client, Mrs Sheila Moore, a sister of the renowned socialite Mrs Pamela Harriman, currently American Ambassador to France. The sisters had a distinguished family background. Their father was an English aristocrat and a fine horseman, Lord Digby. He was Lord Lieutenant of Dorset and Master of the Cattistock Foxhounds. Both he and Lady Digby were legendary for their love of horses and of hunting. The story is told of how Sheila, as a child, had a bad fall while out hunting and was carried home unconscious. When their mother Constance finally returned from the hunt, Pamela indignantly asked her why she had not come straight home with her children, seeing as how her sister Sheila had been hurt. 'Come home,' replied an astonished Lady Digby, 'and miss the best run of the season?'

Lord and Lady Digby's love of horses was passed on to their daughters. Pamela Harriman, who was formerly married to Randolph Churchill, son of the wartime British premier Sir Winston Churchill, still likes to ride showjumpers although in her seventies. Her work as ambassador in one of the most prestigious diplomatic postings in the world, however, doesn't allow her a great deal of time to spend with her horses. Her sister Sheila can afford to take a more leisurely approach to equine matters, and breeds horses on her land at Mallow, Co. Cork. Mrs Moore lives for part of the year on her Irish estate, her home there being a fine Georgian mansion, situated by the banks of the River Blackwater. The rest of her time is spent at her home in Atlanta, Georgia.

Mrs Moore and her late husband Charles bought the Co. Cork estate in 1969, and the following year brought over five mares from America. All the horses she has had in training in Ireland since then have been the progeny of those mares. She had horses for some time with Irish trainer Adrian Maxwell, who, in his younger days, rode at least one winner for Paddy Mullins. But when Adrian went to America she had to find another trainer and plumped for Paddy Mullins. She had never met him but had heard about him. 'Everybody has heard of Paddy,' she says. Mrs Moore just phoned him one day, and Paddy came down to her place in Mallow to look over the horses and to see which ones would be taken into training. He trained some horses for her for the Flat, but she has had more success with the National Hunt horses that have been in training at Doninga in recent years. Mrs Moore is a regular figure at Cheltenham and Aintree. Whenever she's in Ireland, she also makes sure to attend at whatever Irish racecourse where her horses happen to be running.

Back in Atlanta, Mrs Moore is one of the 'placing judges' at the Atlanta Steeplechase races who monitor the finishing line and decide the results. She is an expert on breeding, and on racehorses in general, but when it comes to placing horses in races, she always defers to her trainer's judgement. She laughs as she remarks, 'Paddy is quite a character. He does what he wants. When I asked him some time ago if one of the horses should go to Cheltenham, he looked at me and said, "Where's Cheltenham?"' Mrs Moore is more than happy with the results the Doninga trainer has been getting for her in recent years. One of her horses with Paddy, Notcomplainingbut, ran a good race in the Aintree meeting of April 1995, coming fourth in the Glenlivet Hurdle, and managing to pick up some prize money. During the previous year Notcomplainingbut scored two wins, including the Denny's Juvenile Hurdle at Leopardstown. Another of Mrs Moore's horses, Fabulist, scored two wins during 1994. Archduchess has also been a winner for Mrs Moore.

One of the most successful of all the Moore horses at Doninga has been Force Seven, who had a fantastic season during 1993, scoring five wins while being partnered by Paddy's daughter Sandra, Adrian Maguire, T.P. Treacy and, on two occasions, by Trevor Horgan. 'Unfortunately,' says Mrs Moore, 'Force Seven was unlucky during 1994. She started off favourite in a race at Punchestown but was struck into by another horse. Charlie Swan was riding her – it wasn't his fault.' The mare didn't race for a while but the treatment for her injury was successful and she ran in hurdle races in early 1995. On Easter Monday that year, she ran quite well in the Irish Grand National at Fairyhouse. Ridden by Timmy Murphy she came in fifth behind Flashing Steel, owned by former Taoiseach (Irish Prime Minister) Charles J. Haughey.

Mrs Moore also has some horses with Adrian Maxwell at The Curragh since his return from America. She says her sister Pamela in the US Embassy in Paris, with whom she keeps in regular touch by phone, is always delighted when the horses in Ireland do well. Mrs Moore considers Paddy a terrific trainer. 'He's very shy, and I don't think he likes owners calling around too often, but when you get to know him he has a great sense of humour.' She added with a smile, 'Paddy doesn't tell you a lot – but we get on very well.'

* * *

Among the other Mullins horses that made an impact during the 1990s must be counted Minorette's Girl. Paddy's daughter Sandra rode Minorette's Girl into third place behind Goin On in the Seagram Supreme National Hunt Race at the Cheltenham Festival in 1990, a year that saw the stable turn out an impressive total of 75 winners. Randaka, owned by Martyn J. McEnery, a stud farm owner who bred Red Rum, won three races during that year and went on to be a real money-spinner in succeeding years. Paddy Mullins has vivid memories of riding point-to-point horses for McEnery's father back in the old days. Boro Smackeroo, bred by Mrs Charmian Hill and owned by her son Jeremy, opened the 1991 season with a win and went on during the year to notch up three more successes. Another prolific winner for the stable that year was David Brennan's Mounamara. During the year, Minorette's Girl put up a great performance while being ridden by Tony Mullins to finish second to Crystal Spirit in the Sun Alliance Novice Hurdle at the Cheltenham Festival. The strike rate for the year was 41 winners, the last one of the year coming on 28 December at Leopardstown when Oh What, owned and bred by Mrs Maureen Mullins, and trained by Paddy was ridden to victory by his son Tony.

The year 1992 produced 43 winners for the stable, and Buck's Choice opened the 1993 season by taking the Slaney Hurdle at Naas on 2 January, with Tony riding. Five days later, Camden Buzz, owned by Carmel Byrne, took the Martinstown Bumper at Punchestown with Tom in the saddle. Paddy had a very high regard for Camden Buzz. He says, 'Horses like Camden Buzz develop very slowly. Consequently they are able to beat the handicapper much more so than horses that show rapid improvement.' Camden Buzz took another bumper at Fairyhouse with Tom up and then won a maiden hurdle at Gowran, with Charlie Swan riding. Charlie won another hurdle at Punchestown in April and then Camden Buzz gave Paddy yet another Galway Hurdle success when winning at the festival meeting on 29 July. Camden Buzz went on to win the Smithwicks Hurdle at the Listowel meeting in September but sadly, when the horse was taken home by his owner, he became ill and died. The season ended as it had opened, with a win for Buck's Choice. The horse, ridden by Jason Titley, took the Lucey Feeds Novice Chase at Limerick on 28 December. The year 1993 produced 55 winners.

During the following year, one of the good horses in the stable, Baden, was retired to stud. Baden, a mare, was owned by Swiss bloodstock agent Max Hauri, a son of the man of the same name who used to buy horses for the Swiss army from

Paddy Mullins's father. Back in the late 1970s and early 1980s, Paddy had also trained Baden's dam, St Moritz, for Max Hauri. At Easter 1994 Baden won a charity race at Fairyhouse, ridden by the showjumper Marion Hughes, whose sister is married to Paddy's son Tom. It was Marion's first ride in a race, and her father Seamus was among those who celebrated afterwards with champagne. Tragically, Seamus Hughes shortly afterwards died in Switzerland where he had gone to see his daughter win a showjumping event. Baden was found to have leg trouble and it was decided that she would not race any more, but that she could become a good brood mare. The stable had a total of 48 winners during 1994. At the Cheltenham Festival the following year, Paddy's son Willy kept the family name up by saddling Tourist Attraction, winner of the first event on the first day, the Citroen Supreme Novices Hurdle.

* * *

Veteran BBC commentator Peter O'Sullevan had a brief chat with Paddy Mullins when they met by chance before the Martell Aintree Hurdle at the April 1995 meeting in Aintree. The two men have known each other for a long time and there is a strong mutual respect between them. Paddy's charge Boro Eight was about to take on the Irish super-horse Danoli in this valuable 2 mile 4 furlong race. Paddy remarked to Peter how people thought he was mad to bring Boro Eight over to Liverpool to take on such formidable opposition in the event. Apart from Danoli, the six-horse field included Large Action, who had finished second in the Champion Hurdle and was joint 2–1 favourite with Danoli, and Doran's Pride, winner of the Bonusprint Stayers Hurdle at Cheltenham the previous month, who started at 100–30. Boro Eight was very much the outsider at 33–1, although some shrewd Irish punters backed him each way at 60–1. Paddy was surprised that very few people, either among the public or among the pundits, seemed to give Boro Eight any chance at all.

Boro Eight provided a direct link back to Mrs Hill. She had

bred Boro Eight and the horse had been owned by her son Jeremy until one of Paddy's major clients came up with the price that Jeremy was looking for. The horse was duly sold to the client, Hudson Valley Equine Incorporated, a US company run by a publicity-shy Irish business tycoon living in America. Paddy has given him the nickname 'Hudson Valley'. Boro Eight had won his first bumper in January 1992, ridden by Tom Mullins, following this with another success at Leopardstown ten days later. Boro Eight went on to notch up a series of wins. Adrian Maguire partnered the horse in one particular win at Gowran and was extremely impressed by the animal's performance. Paddy remembers the expression Maguire used when he came in after the race, 'This is a serious horse.' Paddy reckoned that if Boro Eight could reproduce something of the speed he showed at Gowran that day, he should be able to give a good account of himself against Danoli at Aintree.

While many of the pundits gave Boro Eight very little chance in the Aintree event, at least the Irish jockey on the day, Norman Williamson, had faith in the horse. Williamson's agent, seeing that the horse had not been 'jocked', phoned up Paddy some time before the race and asked if Williamson could have the ride. Paddy said he would check with the owner. He knew that 'Hudson Valley' had become friendly with a particular jockey and might be asking for this man to partner Boro Eight. In fact 'Hudson Valley' was more than happy to have Williamson ride. After all, Williamson had more or less dominated the proceedings at the Cheltenham Festival the previous month, riding Alderbrook to win the Champion Hurdle, partnering Putty Road to win the Sun Alliance and then going on to take Master Oats to victory in the Gold Cup.

Danoli, ridden by Charlie Swan, confirmed himself as Ireland's top hurdler by winning the Martell Aintree Hurdle, but unfortunately the horse was injured in the process. Boro Eight, for his part, did Paddy Mullins proud, running a blinder and mounting a late challenge to come second, just three-quarters of a length behind Danoli. Large Action was third and Doran's Pride fourth. Paddy Mullins was extremely pleased by the result, having once more confounded the sceptics. But if he was pleased, the owners, who could not be present on the day, were ecstatic. Apart from the glory of winning, there was some very acceptable prize money for second place – £11,518. Says Paddy, '"Hudson Valley" was on Cloud Nine.'

It was a good result for one small region of the Carlow-Kilkenny countryside. Paddy and Danoli's trainer, Tom Foley have known each other for many years. They are neighbours, living on opposite sides of the River Barrow, just a few miles apart. Tom used to have a mare in training with Paddy, and the two men often meet at the races and talk horses. On a couple of occasions, at Tom's request, Paddy arranged for his own stable jockey T. P. Treacy to ride Danoli. One of the first people to phone Doninga to pass on his congratulations over Boro Eight's showing at Aintree was Jeremy Hill. Says Paddy, 'He was absolutely delighted that Boro Eight had done so well.'

There was also a Kilkenny connection when Jason Titley won the Grand National on the same afternoon as Danoli and Boro Eight competed against each other. Jason Titley had, of course, ridden in a number of races for Paddy before emigrating to England. The Jenny Pitman-trained Royal Athlete whom he rode to victory in the Grand National had been bred by one of Paddy's longest-standing clients, John Brophy, the trainer's second cousin. John was the owner of Luska, who won the Irish Grand National in 1981. Paddy remembers being over at John's farm one evening, looking at horses and discussing a mare called Darjoy. The mare had originally been earmarked to breed showjumpers, but after John and Paddy discussed the matter, it was decided that racehorses could be bred from her. Darjoy was sent to the stallion Roselier, the sire of Carvill's Hill, and the progeny was Royal Athlete, who a few years later was to go on to win Aintree's most famous steeplechase at 40–1.

Epilogue

After more than a half century involved in training horses, Paddy Mullins still puts in a full day's work at his yard in Doninga. Part of his daily routine is to observe the riding out on the gallops. His son Tom drives a rotovator over the six furlong course early in the morning, smoothing out the surface before the arrival of the horses. The gallops are expensive to maintain, costing several thousand pounds every year in materials alone. Paddy drives out from the yard at the back of his house in his Toyota car. He drives up to a wide gate, nudges it open with the car bumper, and proceeds along a farm track to the big field where the gallops are located. In recent times he was mystified to find the gate constantly open. All the lads insisted they had closed it. Then he kept watch, and discovered that one of the horses left out in the fields had worked out a way of undoing the rope used to secure the gate, in order to get to the yard where feedstuffs are stored.

To visitors from the city, the gallops at Doninga on a fine sunny day seem like a marvellous environment in which to work. There is rolling countryside all around, hedgerows, tall trees, woodlands, great views, a sense of wide open spaces. But the riders are keen to remind you that they have to work the horses in good weather and in bad, and that it's not always pleasant. Paddy usually has a pair of binoculars on the back seat of the car, but his eyesight is good, and mostly he doesn't need to use the glasses as he observes his horses going through their paces. His shrewd, experienced eye can pick up how a horse is progressing in training as the animal is ridden around the track. Near the gallops there is a hurdle, and a fence, for schooling horses over the jumps. Paddy doesn't believe in having a series of jumps for young horses to negotiate. He believes that if a horse starting out on his career is schooled over just one obstacle, the animal will all the more quickly gain confidence.

The day's work starts at about 8 o'clock. The horses are fed and the stables are mucked out. Says Paddy, 'Horses are put on the walker first. That's a thing we did not have in the old days. They are ridden out in lots. The first lot goes down to the gallops at about 8.45 and the second goes out about 10 o'clock or a little before. Those involved in the riding out have a break then – it might be a quarter of an hour, it might be longer, and then they get out another lot about 11 o'clock and possibly another lot about 12.30 or 1 o'clock. There is a break for lunch then. Horses are let off in paddocks for a roll after they are ridden, and later taken in from the paddock. The horses get a mid-day feed, and in the afternoon they are brushed over. There are horses that are always being broken or not doing very much and they tend to be left until the afternoon. The lads get the whole yard brushed down and done over and everything tidied up before 5 o'clock. Later on in the night we feed the horses again, any of them that need it.

'Everybody around the place who is able to ride, rides them out – like Tom, T. P. Treacy. There would be days then when they would take horses away to work them on a racecourse or somewhere else. But it would have to be fitted into the daily routine.'

The long white-walled two-storey dwelling house where Paddy and his wife Maureen reared five children is not only a comfortable home – it is also the nerve centre of a major horse training operation. The long comfortable drawing room where an open fire blazes constantly in winter features many mementos of many racing victories, including some very fine pieces of Waterford Glass. Paddy has an office in a house next door, and a secretary, but most often he is to be found at a table in the drawing room poring over racing calendars and form books and records, planning the campaign of his horses, choosing the best races for them. On a nearby table, in the midst of a fine collection of cut glass trophies, there is a Minitel computer which is used for keeping in touch with entries for races. There are plenty of books in evidence, mostly about racing or horses. The phone rings constantly. There are always calls from owners and these can come from many different parts of the world.

In this same room are to be seen racing prints and racing memorabilia, and photos that recall racing history, and the role of the Mullins family in that history. Under glass on a coffee table in front of the fire, for instance, there is a selection of photos that includes a picture of Maureen Mullins with Queen Elizabeth, the Queen Mother, taken at Cheltenham when Dawn Run won the Gold Cup in 1986. Another photo shows Paddy talking to Princess Anne at the unveiling of a statue of Dawn Run. There are many trophies around this room, which is like a shrine to Irish racing history. Paddy is particularly proud of a small model of an Etruscan warrior that stands on the mantelpiece. It was awarded to him to mark the year that he was leading trainer, his son Willy was top amateur NH jockey, and his other son Tony was top professional.

Every night, the last thing Paddy Mullins does is to check over the horses himself. He enters each stable, patting the horses, whispering to them, feeling a tendon here or a fetlock there, straightening a sheet, and allowing his experienced eye and his instinct to tell him if all is well – or not well as the case might be. If any of the horses need extra food, he will provide that. So how does he know when they need extra feed? Says Paddy: 'They don't eat up everything when they get it. The evening feed is the big feed and they take hours to clean it up. Some of them will gobble it up straight away but they would be the exception. They are picking at it and picking at it and if it's completely cleaned up I will say, well maybe you will eat another little bit and I will give it to them. But mostly they don't eat everything that's flung into them. Then when they go asleep they lie down and stretch out. They lie on their side and they are relaxed and that's what I love to see.' Sometimes, when his nightly tour of the stables is over, Paddy likes to read. The books can be of any kind – fiction or non-fiction. His favourite author is P. G. Wodehouse.

It has not always been an easy life. Tony Mullins says, 'The secret of my father's success is his ability to stay going in good or bad times. No matter how difficult things might have been he would keep going and going. When others were ready to give up, he would still stay at it. I'm starting to believe now it's the secret of a lot of people's success in life.'

Now that her family is reared, Maureen is heavily involved in the administrative side of the running of the stable, and she still rides out every day. Maureen is very much an extrovert, and is very good at dealing with the stable's clientele. Maureen and Paddy have always been devoted to their family and they now dote on their grandchildren.

There are about 40 horses in training in the yard, and about a dozen lads employed, the head man being John English. Up to May 1995, after 42 years of training horses under his own licence, Paddy Mullins has recorded more than 1,550 winners. It is, as he says himself, the result of a life with horses. Now aged 76, he is regarded as the doyen of Irish trainers, and has no plans to retire. Who knows what more surprises he may have in store for the racing world – another Champion Hurdle, another Gold Cup?

The support of a close-knit family is clearly of the utmost importance to him. His family – and his horses – seem to keep him young, quick-witted and full of vigour. 'My life has been with horses,' he says simply. 'I could not imagine myself living without them . . . '

Appendix

DAWN RUN'S RECORD

Dawn Run, foaled 1978, by Deep Run – Twilight Slave

Date	Venue	Race Description	Jockey	Place
29.5.82	Clonmel	Corinthian INH Race	Mrs C.D. Hill	8th
17.6.82	Thurles	Devils Bit INH Flat Race	Mrs C.D. Hill	4th
22.6.82	Tralee	Castlemaine INH Flat Race	Mrs C.D. Hill	won
31.7.82	Galway	Tonroe INH Flat Race	Mr T. Mullins	won
2.9.82	Tralee	Havasnack Flat Race	Mr T. Mullins	won
13.11.82	Leo'town	November Handicap	P.V. Gilson	16th
27.11.82	Naas	Kilwarden Maiden Hurdle	P. Kavanagh	4th
20.12.82	Navan	Blackhills Maiden Hurdle	A. Mullins	won
28.12.82	Leo'town	Findus Beefburger Hurdle	A. Mullins	won
29.1.83	Leo'town	Delgany Hurdle	A. Mullins	6th
5.2.83	Pun'town	Fournoughts Hurdle	A. Mullins	won
19.2.83	F'house	Monaloe H'cap Hurdle	A. Mullins	3rd

16.3.83	Chelt'ham	Sun Alliance Hurdle	R. Barry	2nd
8.4.83	Liverpool	Page Three Hurdle	A. Mullins	won
9.4.83	Liverpool	Sun Templegate Hurdle	A. Mullins	2nd
26.4.83	Pun'town	BMW Champion Hurdle	A. Mullins	won
22.10.83	Curragh	Giolla Mear Flat Race	P. V. Gilson	4th
5.11.83	Down Royal	A. R. Soudavar Trial Hurdle	A. Mullins	won
18.11.83	Ascot	VAT Watkins Hurdle	J. J. O'Neill	won
7.12.83	Naas	Racehorse Trainers' Hurdle	J. J. O'Neill	2nd
26.12.83	Kempton	Christmas Hurdle	J. J. O'Neill	won
18.2.84	Leo'town	Wessel Champion Hurdle	J. J. O'Neill	won
13.3.84	Chelt'ham	Champion Hurdle	J. J. O'Neill	won
31.3.84	Liverpool	Sandeman Aintree Hurdle	A. Mullins	won
28.5.84	Auteuil	Prix La Barka	A. Mullins	won
22.6.84	Auteuil	Grande Course de Haies	A. Mullins	won
1.11.84	Navan	Nobber Chase	A. Mullins	won
14.12.85	Pun'town	Durkan Bros Chase	A. Mullins	won
30.12.85	Leo'town	Sean P. Graham Chase	A. Mullins	won
25.1.86	Chelt'ham	Holsten Distributors Chase	A. Mullins	4th
13.3.86	Chelt'ham	Tote Gold Cup	J. J. O'Neill	won
3.4.86	Liverpool	Whitbread Gold Label Cup	J. J. O'Neill	fell
23.4.86	Pun'town	Match	A. Mullins	won
2.6.86	Auteuil	Prix La Barka	A. Mullins	2nd
27.6.86	Auteuil	Grande Course de Haies	M. Chirol	fell

Index

INDEX

INDEX

Nicholson, David 'The Duke', 15,
65–6, 69–70, 103
Nicholson, Dinah, 65
Nicholson, 'Frenchie', 65
Nicholson, Tom, 39, 41, 59, 110
Nicolaus Silver, 51–2
Nijinsky, 71
Nor, 70–2
Norton, Clody (Hall-Dare), 50, 65,
71–2

O'Brien, Dr Bill, 24
O'Brien, Dr Vincent, 27, 52, 65, 157,
173
O'Connor, Tim, 174–5
O'Dwyer, Conor, 175–6
Oh What, 210
O'Leary, Jarlath, 191–2
O'Leary, Margaret, 192–4
O'Leary, Tom, 191–4
O'Neill, Ann, 83
O'Neill, Harry, 103
O'Neill, Jerry, 53, 75–6
O'Neill, Jonjo:, 11, 12, 128, 132–3,
137–9, 150–2, 155, 164, 187
O'Neill, Peter, 174
O'Riordan, Joe, 152
O'Riordan, Pat, 152
O'Sullevan, Peter, 151, 211
Onions, Tony, 41, 110
Osborne, Joe ,46
Oxx, John, 52

Painter's Cottage, 54
Palmer, Col M. F., 57
Pariglit, 188
Parijatak, 96, 186–7
Parnell, Buster, 53, 71, 73–4
Parnell, David, 74, 181
Perrot, Jacques, 187
Piggott, Lester, 56, 71–2, 83–4, 113
Pipe, Martin, 185–6
Pitman, Jenny, 175–6, 213
Pitman, Mark, 176
Prendergast, Kevin, 42
Prendergast, P. J. 'Darkie', 42, 52
Pretty Polly Stakes, 87
Prix de l'Arc de Triomphe, 88–9
Prix des Drags, 67–8
Prix La Barka, 142–3, 158
Prix Vermeille, 88

Raining, 52
Redundant Pal, 171–7
Rimell, Fred, 51
Riordan, John, 111
Riordan, Prudence, 111

Robinson, G. W., 42, 56
Roe, Johnny, 53, 70, 87, 187, 194
Ronayne, Michael, 79
Royal Athlete, 213
Ruane, Tom, 81
Rudkin, Dotsie, 78–80, 93
Rudkin, Henry (Jnr), 78–80, 93
Rudkin, Henry (Snr), 77–8
Rudkin, Margaret, 77–8

St Moritz, 211
Sayparee, 185–6
Scally Owen, 172–3
Scott, Brough, 144
Scudamore, Peter, 15, 161, 179–80,
185–6
Secret Venture, 58
Sharif, Omar, 117, 119
Silver Road, 93–5
Simpson, Alan, 71
Sleator, Paddy, 27, 52
Smithwick, Joe, 51
Solwezi, 54, 56
Some Chicken, 33
Straker, Ivan, 185
Street Angel, 124
Swan, Charlie, 141, 212

Thackeray, William Makepeace, 17, 21
Thompson, Brent, 148
Thorpe, Dr Malcolm, 83–9
Titley, Jason, 210, 213
Tradehimin, 180, 182
Treacy, Jim, 109
Treacy, Sean, 55, 108–9
Treacy, T. P., 55, 213, 216
Turf Club, 11, 131

Vigors, A. C., 199
Vigors, Terence, 24, 199
Vulpine, 22, 58–60

Walsh, Sean, 178
Walsh, Ted, 79
Ward, Liam, 71
Wells, Georgie, 62
Whatever, 41–2
Wildenstein, Daniel, 84, 145–6
Williamson,Norman, 16, 182, 212
Wilson, Diana, 61
Wilson, James, 61–2, 69–70
Wilson, Noreen, 61–2, 64, 67–9
Wilson, Robbie, 61
Winter, Fred, 61
Wylie, Judge, W. E. 39

Yrrah Jr, 86

224